D0604063

. . .

For twelve years, I tossed and toiled with you (book) and you always made me feel like I was never enough. Here you are, in all your glory, and none of it could have been done without all of the support I received from others along the way.

To Reyna, Isabel, LuLu, and Ava—you are my heart, my family, and my life—you have always made me feel like I was more than enough.

- DAVE

www.mascotbooks.com

The Dot on the Left

I have tried to recreate events, locales, and conversations from my memories of them. In order to maintain their anonymity in some instances, I have changed the names of individuals and places. I may have changed some identifying characteristics and details such as physical properties, occupations, and places of residence.

For more information, please contact:
Mascot Books
560 Herndon Parkway #120
Herndon, VA 20170
info@mascotbooks.com

Library of Congress Control Number: 2017909201

CPSIA Code: PBANG1017A
ISBN-13: 978-1-68401-415-6

Printed in the United States

the
dot on
the left

DAVE SWANSON

I first started talking with Dave Swanson in 2005, not long after he'd returned home from a year of combat in Baghdad. I was neck deep in a research project that ultimately turned into my book, In a Time of War, about West Point and the wars in Iraq and Afghanistan. I had been a lawyer in the Army JAG Corps, but the truth is that a lot of things have to go really, really wrong before a JAG officer winds up in an actual firefight. Now, I was now getting a crash course in combat leadership through the men and women of the U.S. Military Academy Class of 2002.

From the beginning, Dave was different. I had been introduced to a long line of impressive officers and West Point graduates as a result of my project. Many of them had the kind of pedigrees that would have made them competitive students at any top-ranked college. There were high school class presidents and valedictorians, team captains and debate champions among them. Upon graduation, they were the new lieutenants who were sent to learn real-life leadership in the Army's most storied units. Or else, they were offered overseas sabbaticals, studying at Oxford as Rhodes Scholars or exploring concepts that would earn them advanced degrees in other parts of the world, before taking their place as junior military commanders.

Not Dave, though. Nothing seemed to have come easy to him. As you will learn on these pages, even just getting to R-Day at West Point had been an arduous journey for him. This was not a guy who had been voted "most likely to succeed" in high school, or at West Point for that matter. The very first draft of the story that I wrote culminated with how he got a big parking ticket during his graduation ceremony—what other West Point graduate would have that happen, never mind remember it when talking with an interviewer years later? But as I got to know Dave better and learned more about his story, two things became clear.

First, he passed what I call "the lead brother test" with flying colors. That means that if I had a little brother who joined the Army, and I learned that Dave was going to be his commander in combat, I'd be okay with that. I saw that he had a rare combination of attributes: an ability to connect with and care for his troops on an individual level, coupled with a hard-nosed ability to make decisions and act.

Second, I realized that while I respected and became grateful for all the time that more than hundreds of soldiers and others gave me while I was writing *In a Time of War*, Dave was one of a handful of graduates whose interviews I truly looked forward to. He was simply a good guy with a sense of humor and a sense of perspective—someone who could tell a good story, and who became a friend, too.

Looking back at some of my notes and interview transcripts now, more than a decade after I first met Dave, I'm struck by a few things. First, I'm reminded of the sheer scope of combat that Dave led his men through—a scale that was rare at the time and still stands out today, with more than 100 days in a row where he was engaged in at least one firefight. And second, I'm struck by how short a time had passed since the fighting, at least at the time we talked. This was a person who not long before had led troops in combat, suffered casualties, and resigned himself to the idea that he would not be coming home alive. Yet, here he was, recounting his stories to a journalist he'd never met in person at the time, and doing so with humor and depth for hours at a time.

All of this made Dave into a great character in my book. But there's more to the story. If you're looking for a role model as you try to make a change in your life—if you're the type of person who hopes to turn an ordinary background into an extraordinary outcome—I think Dave's story will resonate with you.

The theme is something like, "Where you start in life is not where you have to end up." In fact, with the benefit of hindsight, the end might look nothing at all like the beginning.

In the years since *In a Time of War* was published, I've had the opportunity to spend a lot of time doing deep dives on questions of leadership and success. I've gone on to write several more books (mostly about entrepreneurship), and started several companies. I also write constantly about these subjects for Inc. com, where I have one of the top columns, and I wind up often using Dave as an example.

His is an example of how to control your fear when times get tough, and to remain focused on achieving your goals when mayhem surrounds you—of selfless leadership and self-reliance, and pushing yourself to your limits.

The Dot on the Left teaches us that exceptionalism isn't something you're born with, it's something you work for—resilience is a daily exercise and leadership a practiced art.

—Bill Murphy Jr., August 2017

•ACKNOWLEDGMENTS•

Let me thank my family for their support, for their belief in me, and for pushing me to be my best. My parents, George and Becky Swanson—you made me stronger than I ever thought I could be in this life.

My wife, Reyna, and daughters, Isabel, Lulu, and Ava—your belief in me is more than anything I have ever asked for in a family.

To my sister, Erica, and my brother, Brian—you make me as driven today as you did when I was a kid.

To Tom—your editing skills are beyond belief, and I'm not sure where I would be without you in this journey.

To Mascot Books—Naren and team—I can't say enough thanks for the professionalism throughout the collaboration to make this book a success.

Thanks Clint—this all started with your advice.

To the Prepsters out there from '98 —you were all there for me, even if you didn't know it.

Finally, Charles (Chuck, Woody) Woodruff—thanks for taking me on and being my mentor. I don't care what you say—I am forever in debt for what you did for me, and I will always be here for you if you ever need me.

Without God (and spaghetti) none of this would have been possible. Sing hymnal. Now.

one
•ARRIVAL•

. . .

"Stay-stay with us!-rest!-thou art weary and worn!
And fain was their war-broken soldier to stay;
But sorrow return'd with the dawning of morn,
And the voice in my dreaming ear melted away."

- FRANCIS T. PALGRAVE

Have you ever had a life-changing moment? What about a life-changing year? Sometimes, after completing an especially arduous task, I have wondered, "How did I make it through that?" I'm sure you have, too. For me, I can point to one particularly transformative experience that has helped me navigate one test after another in the years since I endured it—from being a part of more than one hundred firefights in Iraq to bicycling across the country and climbing a serious glacier in Mt. Rainier, from graduating from the U.S. Military Academy to receiving an MBA from the University of Texas and pursuing a Ph.D. in leadership from Concordia College Chicago (while pursing my career in the private sector full-time). This memorable experience taught me how to tackle any challenge and provided me with the confidence to face just about any obstacle without backing down. It transformed me from someone who wonders, "Can I do this?" into someone who simply says, "I will do this." It taught me lessons I use every day of my life.

I wrote this book to share the lessons from that year and to talk to you about one critical takeaway that is at the core of my experience. That takeaway is this: we all have dreams, but only some of us turn them into actual goals that we truly pursue with the effort they require—and even fewer of us manage to make them a reality. We all daydream, but too often we only fool ourselves into thinking they will somehow magically just happen. This story is about how that magic really happens: perseverance, grit, and support from others.

In my experience, dreams, goals, and realities do not happen without support from the people around us. It would be great, wouldn't it, to be able to look back from the top of a mountain and yell, "I did this! All on my own without any help!" Those are silly words, and it's crazy to ever think that we accomplish anything great in this life on our own. Let's dispel the thought that I achieved anything in this book on my own without all of the amazing people around me. This book is as much about them and the support they provided as it is about my own personal journey.

I want to challenge you with this book in one specific way. After you've finished reading, I want you to create a sense of urgency about that dream you've always had. Stop waiting for it to happen and make it a goal that you authentically chase every day. And, then, finally, I want you to make it a reality. After all, remember these wise words:

Out there things can happen, and frequently do,
To people as brainy and footsy as you.
And when things start to happen, don't worry, don't stew.
Just go right along, you'll start happening too!
- *Oh, the Places You'll Go!* by Dr. Seuss

Dr. Seuss is a magical source of insight, not just for children but for all of us. The definition of success means a lot of things to a lot of people. Never define yourself with the measure of what someone else defines as success. To me, success means never quitting on something I am passionate about. That's it. It's about the chase—the headlong pursuit of something important to me. It's not the accumulation of degrees, cars, houses, money, or anything else. It's not tangible.

Of course, we all have our own goals that are important to us. Before I showed up at the United States Military Academy Prep School, my goal was the acceptance of my peers. Once I started at the school, my simple goal was to make it through each day. Eventually, my dreams grew more ambitious and so did my goals, such as graduating from the United States Military Academy, perhaps the most demanding institution of higher education in the country. My dreams, goals, and realities changed over time, but I never gave up on them, no matter what they were. Ultimately, my understanding that this was the true measure of success started in Prep School.

The purpose of the United States Military Academy Preparatory School, also known as USMAPS, the Prep School, or West Point Prep, is to prepare selected candidates for admission to the United States Military Academy at West Point. The U.S. Military Academy Preparatory School was formally established in 1946. Thirty years earlier, Congress had enacted legislation authorizing the appointment of former enlisted soldiers to West Point, where they could earn commissions as officers. The Prep School was designed to ease this transition, and today its students include not only soldiers but also civilians straight out of high school, most of them athletes who need extra academic help before taking on the challenges of the Academy. As a result, West Point Prep is primarily an academic institution that accepts students and soldiers from diverse backgrounds and challenges them over the course of a year to meet and exceed West Point's rigorous admission standards.

As an enlisted soldier applying to West Point, I had little chance of going directly there, nor did I want to make that leap after hearing about the Academy's stringent academics. The other candidates at the Prep School were people who would be going through the same experience as I would, and I knew we would form strong bonds as the year progressed. I took comfort in this knowledge as I entered the West Point system and had my first encounter with the other candidates and the officers in charge of me.

When I arrived that first day, I remember whispering to myself, "This is the biggest mistake of my life," as I approached the gates of the ostensible hell that distinguished my future from just about everyone else's in the world. I only told myself that because I was scared. I didn't know what to expect, and everyone discouraged me from applying, saying it was a big mistake. Sometimes, repeating other people's words to ourselves can be more damaging than anything we hear. Hell to me was Fort Monmouth, New Jersey, where the school was located. I had been accepted to the prestigious school, but it felt as if I was the only one who didn't refer to it as a "complete waste of a year."

However, deep down I knew that this wasn't a mistake—it was an opportunity of epic proportions. I felt I would have the greatest year of my life and be catapulted into becoming the kind of adept leader I had always thought I could be. Reframing my mental attitude required my own input of a situation to overcome the influence of other people.

It was the end of July 1997, and the East Coast's humidity was melting the black polish off the boots that paced the sidewalks. I could tell that area beautification was important here—the manicured bushes and neatly edged sidewalks highlighting the school's surroundings. This was going to be serious.

All candidates arrived in civilian clothes. This bothered the tactical non-commissioned officers (TAC NCOs) in charge, because the majority of us were already in the United States Army. Some of the new students had not been in the Army, however, and neither had their parents. Until these moms and dads stopped milling around the post, the TAC NCOs had to be polite.

I couldn't help but wonder where my parents were and if they even supported the idea of my attending the Prep School. When I had signed on the dotted line with the Army recruiter in March of 1995, my mother said, "You just wasted your life, boy." Little did we know that the soldier's life ahead would provide me the opportunity to attend one of the most prestigious universities in the world. My parents' support had always been there throughout high school, but joining the Army was a big step. As with any kid, I just wanted my parents to be proud of me. For anything. They were ignorant to the idea of West Point. Hell, I was in the Army, and I had never even heard of the Academy until I was at my Advanced Individual Training (AIT) in Pensacola, Florida.

I had enlisted straight out of high school at the age of seventeen, eager to get out of the small town of Owensville, Ohio, where I grew up. I joined the Army Reserves as a private with hopes of attending a junior college so I could get my grades up while playing basketball. Basketball had been the priority in my life for so long that many other areas had always taken the backseat. Academics were more of a distraction in my mind, rather than something that would help me achieve the goals I had set. I soon realized I needed more help with my studies than I had originally thought. Looking back now, it is astonishing to me that I failed junior college but completed the Academy's distinguished academics.

My first Army assignment after basic training was AIT for Army photography and video. I had told the entrance station recruiters that I would take any job in the Army with the stipulation that I didn't want to use my intellect. I had scored fairly high on the general technical portion of the ASVAB test (the military entrance aptitude exam), and I knew there were many options available to me when it came to selecting a job.

The first job that popped up was photography, and I happily chose it. While at AIT in Florida, I learned to volunteer for community projects and received my first taste of leadership. I liked these leadership opportunities, and I loved the challenges.

I can remember standing in front of a platoon of forty privates and specialists of varying ages. I had only been there for three months, but the drill sergeants recognized me as a leader among peers. My first speech was awkward, and I learned quickly what not to say if you want people to follow you.

"Listen up! As long as everyone listens to the orders I put out, we will be fine. If you don't, I have no problems with issuing MFRs (Memorandum For Records) to each and every one of you." Silence. Except one person, who went "PFFT!" I deserved both actually. Over time, I earned trust, person by person, but it wasn't easy. I was never invited to parties or out on the weekends because I was viewed as someone who would report people to the drill sergeants. I learned something with that position: peer leadership is the hardest form of leadership in any organization. I have since led teams of peers in Fortune 500 companies, and, much like in that first platoon, I was always challenged. You have to earn trust before anyone truly wants to work with you. In this position, I also recognized that I wanted to become a leader of soldiers. I was enlisted, and I hadn't considered becoming an officer yet. It wasn't until several months of being in this position that I saw there was an opportunity to become a true leader.

My daytime job as the platoon guide was beginning to level itself out, but I needed to find some additional volunteer work to keep myself busy. I worked with Saturday Scholars, a program dedicated to teaching younger children how to read. During this time, I also found my first volunteer job as a librarian. I chose this job between my photography and video classes because most soldiers decided to be a volunteer at the youth camps for summer. After a short stint of loud children and supervision, I decided that the silence of the library would better suit me.

I spent hours reading the classics of Hemingway, Steinbeck, and J.D. Salinger that I never read in high school. I was introduced to the internet and learned the protocols of the World Wide Web. I felt I was learning more at the library by studying on my own than I would have if I had stayed in junior college. It was the first time I recognized that I enjoyed learning. I had an intellectual curiosity that felt forced when I attended junior college. To me, learning is growing, and I have identified that growing makes me happier and more fulfilled. That hasn't changed for me, even to this day.

During this time at the library, I often saw several brochures arranged on the tables. One day, a friend and I each picked up a pamphlet and read about a school that boasted the ultimate leadership experience. Jeremy Huser was a silly character with dirty blonde hair and thick glasses that would later make drill sergeants laugh during a smoking session of privates.

The promise of leadership challenges at West Point wasn't what first caught my eye, however. Rather, it was the basketball team and the fact that I could go to school for "free."

Jeremy and I both received our applications for the Prep School, but he declined his chance to go because it would take a week to fill out the paperwork and complete the physical tests. I thought he was a fool for not wanting to go through some minor headaches to take a shot at the most difficult school in America. Deep down, however, I rejoiced in his decision not to participate, because I wanted the challenge of getting accepted to be my own. I loved the idea of being challenged and knew I always gave my best regardless of the situation.

The physical aptitude exam for my Prep School application consisted of several tasks. I ran 54 seconds on the shuttle run, tossed the basketball 89 feet, did 15 pull-ups, and completed a broad jump that measured close to 8 feet. I later learned that I was in the 95th percentile with those scores. I was warned, however, that there was something wrong with my heart rate.

The smell of the doctor's office usually creates an unappealing nostalgia for me. The sterility of the floor and the squeaking sounds of nurses' shoes as they scurry up and down the hallways always give me the chills. When I was a child, I spent quite a few hours at doctors' offices and began to hate wasting my time in waiting rooms and pharmacies. My mother dubbed me the "Million Dollar Kid" for the money I cost in medical bills. In fact, I was the only one of the children in my family to need any kind of surgery and to wear glasses and braces. A clandestine "milkman visit" has always been a possibility in the back of my mind. It's no surprise I despised hospitals by the age of eighteen.

At my medical appointment, I found myself waiting impatiently for the doctor. The only thing on my mind was to complete this physical and move on to the next task in the application process, which could take hours to complete. When the doctor finally arrived, he told me that my heart exam showed I not only had an abnormal heartbeat but that my heart was shaped differently. The doctor's first clue was that, in a normal state, my heart rate was thirty-two beats per minute. An average heart rate is between fifty and sixty beats per minute. I informed the doctor that I ran a minimum of five miles a day and played several hours of basketball every night.

Despite my fitness and high level of activity, the doctor was alarmed by the rate of my heartbeat. After the exam, which included an x-ray, he sat me down and told me that most hearts are the size of a fist and are flat. He gave me a demonstration by putting his hand flat out in front of him. Then, he said, "Your heart is more like this." He canted his hand upward and showed what it should have looked like with the other. This, he told me, would probably eliminate me from the school. "I understand that West Point only takes the students in top physical shape, and I don't think that you should report in your condition." His words hit me like rocks.

I begged the doctor, telling him he was about to end my dream of becoming an officer. "If you report this, I will never reach my full potential, and all I've ever wanted to be in life is a leader of soldiers! How can you stop my dream of wanting to be that, sir?" In frustration, I buried my head in my hands.

It was then that he understood that what I wanted to do was more important than any report. With his voice quiet and sincere, he told me, "These exams are for judging whether the service member is ready for the school's activities. West Point should be honored to have people like you wanting to attend their school."

I joyously thanked him, collected the "new" results, and escaped his office before he could change his mind. Many people would have stopped after the heart exam and questioned whether West Point was the right place for them. I never considered not going. I had made the decision in my mind to go after this goal, and I wasn't going to let a minor detail derail me. In life, we do that too often. We get hung up on minor details and treat mere pebbles like boulders and allow them to stop us from achieving our goals. Next time you run into an obstacle that has you feeling dejected, ask yourself, "Is this a pebble or is this a boulder?" Once you have got it accurately sized up, you can formulate a plan to overcome it.

It wasn't the first time that I had caught some luck getting past a medical exam. In fact, something similar had happened when I had first enlisted in the Army. I had gone to the Military Entrance Processing Station (MEPS) for my physical exam. Among the procedures I had undergone when I was a kid was a series of operations putting tubes in my ear to allow fluid to enter and release without affecting my inner ear and balance. So, when it was time for the hearing test, I knew I couldn't pass it. I hadn't really heard out of my left ear since I was thirteen, and I was pretty sure it wasn't going to change that day. We have all been in that booth. They test both ears for noises that range from loud to soft and then test again with background noise. I have taken and failed these tests many times throughout my youth.

I had to get creative. There were six different booths, so I figured the nurses wouldn't be able to see me watching the other patients. When the other patients pressed the button, I pressed mine at the same time. After the exam finished, I heard a message over the PA system. "Number five, please remain in the booth."

I knew from this voice that I had been caught watching the other patients. For the retest, I devised a plan so that when (or if) I could hear the first three sounds, the loudest ones possible, I would count in between the beats and just give it a shot. One ... two ... three. One ... two ... three.

"Number five, you did better than the first time. Good job."

Good job, my ass. I couldn't hear a truck coming through my living room if I was asleep on the couch. I felt good about tricking the nurses on the hearing test, but getting past my vision exam wasn't going to be as easy.

When I reached the vision station next, the optometry nurse asked me to read the sign. I have poor vision—20/600 poor—and one eye even has astigmatism. I knew there would be no way I could see well enough to pass. The nurse told me to read line three on the sign. To read this line without glasses was the Army's minimum requirement. I couldn't cheat my way out of this one because they changed the sign for every patient.

"I'm not going to lie to you," I said, not hiding my sorrow. "I can't even see the board."

With a slow look, side to side, as if she had just committed a crime, the nurse said, "Good job. You passed."

I couldn't argue with her. I wanted to be in the Army, and she was helping me out. It was clear that the Army was only letting in the top physical specimens, and I, somehow, was one of them. I didn't recognize it at the time, but these medical folks helped me out much more than they had to for the screening. I'm not sure why they would do that, maybe it was the ambition on my face or the sense that this had become a dream for me. Either way, there are people like this in all of our lives. In a particular moment, you may not even recognize they are helping you. When you find out, give gratitude for having these people in your life, even if the help seems as small as helping you pass a few medical tests.

At my next test, the Prep School physical exam, I snapped back to my original exam room for the rest of my clothes and thanked the doctor once more for his approval on the heart exam. The rest of the physical consisted of all the normal tests, which I could easily pass, even the rectal exam, which is every young military man's "favorite." I never could figure out why I always got the oldest doctor with shaky hands and a foreign name. "Dr. Janikowski, your next patient, Swanson, is here for his rectal exam." I shook my head at the sight of the old man, but this was my second time, and I had become quite adept at the evaluation.

With the physical tests finished, the hardest things left were the essays. I had never had to write essays that demonstrated my writing ability before, let alone had to write something that would express my interest in the Academy.

I sat alone in an empty barracks room and spent hours writing and rewriting the essays so they would be perfect for the admissions department. The first question, "Why do you want to attend a service academy?" was nerve-wracking, owing to the limited space I had to explain so many things. At first, I closed my eyes and hoped to be motivated by the music playing from my radio. I was. I listened to the song "The Impossible Dream" from the 1996 Summer Olympics soundtrack over and over again while writing all three essays.

I felt inspired by the music, especially because getting into West Point still seemed like an impossible dream based on my academic scores. I've always had a penchant for impossible dreams. There is something about achieving something that everyone around you believes is beyond your abilities. From climbing mountains to running marathons to cycling across the United States, I do these things not only for my own satisfaction but hopefully to inspire other people to go after their dreams as well. I honestly feel that I am an ordinary person of ordinary gifts who just possesses the persistence to keep going, even when failure keeps happening. If I can accomplish something through hard work, so can anyone.

I completed the essays and gave the recommendation sheets to my drill sergeants and my company commander. The commander called me into his office in the fall of 1996 and asked me if I knew what I was doing. He was a prior service officer and a former Marine. He asked if I was ready to handle all of the political bullshit that goes with being an officer in the U.S. Army.

"Sir," I said, "I can handle any bullshit that comes my way as long as I'm not still a private in the Army bullshit."

He laughed at my response and quickly finished the recommendation so I could wait on the admissions department's approval or disapproval. Either way, I was ready to get out of Florida. I wasn't sure if it was the sweltering Pensacola humidity, but I knew life had to be better somewhere else.

I had told my parents about my opportunity to attend West Point, or at least its prep school, and to get paid to do so. I couldn't believe the bargain I was getting. Later, I would learn the meaning of the expression that "the Army would take it all back, with interest, and from my ass a nickel at a time," but for now I thought the whole thing was a sweet deal.

I called my parents after I had completed the application.

"Where is West Point?" my mother asked.

"It's in New York," I told her.

"So, are you going to try and become president?"

What, I wondered, *is she talking about?*

"No," I mumbled. "I'm going there to play basketball and get college paid for."

Her lack of response to that gave me time to wonder, *We had presidents go there?* Although I had taunted my parents for not knowing anything about the school, neither apparently did I. Together, neither one of us really had any in-depth knowledge about West Point and what it truly meant to attend.

After I turned in my application, the process became a waiting game with Col. Jones, director of admissions at West Point. Unfortunately, I had scored 750 on the SATs. 750 total. Not 750 out of the possible 800 on the math portion, which some West Point applicants score, and not 750 on the verbal portion, which others earn. I scored only 750 out of a total of 1600 possible points. That score proved to be a big roadblock.

I was in my Advanced Individual Training school when I received a phone call from Col. Jones. *THE* Col. Jones of admissions, my saint or Satan, wanted to talk to me because he had a few issues with my application that he wanted to smooth over with me.

"There are three things," he told me, "that we look at when accepting someone to the Prep School. Leadership, physical ability, and academics."

I knew which one he wanted to discuss with me. I had a 2.5 GPA in high school, 76th out of a class of 142, the bottom 50 percent. More than 80 percent of the people accepted to West Point, however, were valedictorians and National Honors recipients. I had trouble spelling "valedictorian."

"Son," Col. Jones said, "you're outstanding in every aspect except academics. In fact, your scores and recommendations for leadership are higher than anyone else's who applied."

I heard the concern in his voice, and I understood that the big BUT was about to hit me.

"But," he said, "your schoolwork is atrocious. We analyzed your scores, and no one in the admissions department thinks you can even finish the Prep School curriculum. What do you think about that?"

As a private at that time, I had only been around one colonel in the Army, and I had learned to only speak when beaten with a stick. Here was my chance to tell the Colonel what I thought of his colleagues and the admissions department.

"Sir, you can look at my scores and realize that I didn't do great in school. That is obvious. However, my determination and my perseverance to do well at that school aren't on any application process. If you give me the chance, I will study twenty hours a day if necessary. I will do anything it takes for me to not only finish that school, but to excel there. And if you give me the opportunity to attend the Prep School, I will not only finish there, but West Point as well."

Taken aback a bit, the Colonel took a deep breath. He told me that my confidence would weigh heavily upon the admissions department's decision. I hung up the phone and slumped over. Despite my speech, I felt discouraged and, frankly, that my chance was over. The biggest takeaway from this encounter is that you honestly never know how people are going to react to a discussion. Col. Jones came in with nothing but numbers and scores to evaluate me. When he asked me my thoughts, he was able to put a person to those numbers—to learn something about me that data couldn't tell him. And for some reason, he liked that person.

I waited another five months before I received an answer from Col. Jones and his team.

I had finished my schooling in Pensacola and gone home to Nashville, Tennessee, to see my family—who had moved there from Ohio soon after I graduated high school—before going to Fort Sam Houston in San Antonio, Texas. In my two weeks at home, I checked the mailbox every day except one. That was the day my brother went down the hill to pick up the mail. I saw him walk up with a large yellow package. I was certain it was from West Point. He walked through the door and told me it was for my parents. Another day gone and I began sulking.

But my mother read the top of the envelope and yelled, "It's from the Prep School. It says 'Open Immediately.'"

I tore into the package as if it had been under the tree on Christmas morning, and I guessed it was the long-awaited toy I knew I was going to get. When I read the first line, tears came to my eyes. All of the months of waiting and wondering about my future focused on this moment. Amid a lie from my brother, my mother shouting, and then finally getting to read the letter of acceptance, I was on my way to the United States Military Academy Preparatory School. I could hardly believe it. If I had known what the acceptance meant— the challenges that awaited—I would have seriously reconsidered my options. Instead, I exalted in the news and felt eager to prove to Col. Jones and the admissions department that choosing me was the best decision they had ever made.

two
•FIRST DAY•

...

"Leadership is the art of giving people a platform for spreading ideas that work."

- SETH GODIN

"**D**ump your bags!" Sgt. First Class Sutton barked his orders in a way that made you complete the task as soon as possible. "I said dump your bags NOW!"

Sgt. First Class Sutton was a non-commissioned officer (NCO) who could make grown men cry with a snarl of his voice. He was the epitome of an NCO. At first glance, his starch-soaked BDU's (battle dress uniforms) gave way to his chiseled chest and bulging biceps. There was no doubt in my mind that his seventeen years of push-ups, sit-ups, and running defined his body, but more importantly his character of toughness that would discipline all of us.

As ten of us stood in line with the contents of our bags strewn across the grass, we looked at each other and tried to analyze what kind of place this was going to be. Sgt. First Class Sutton made his way down the line, tossing aside anything that he considered "contraband." It was amazing what qualified. He saw a clock radio, grabbed it, and chucked it about twenty yards. He found a CD player in the possession of a cadet candidate (CC) about three people down from me. "You knew better," he growled, shaking his head. I watched the CD player fly thirty yards. His throwing arm made me believe that he had become quite proficient at this process over the years.

made me believe that he had become quite proficient at this process over the years.

He finally made his way to my gear at the end of the line and considered the items I had emptied onto the grass for his review. He realized I didn't have anything he could take from me.

"Mr. Perfect," he snapped. "I'll have to keep my eyes on you!"

Rather than responding to his taunt, I gathered my things and threw them back into the bags without any regard to their importance. I hurried to the second floor where our names were already posted on the doors of our new homes. We had no choice of roommates. I threw my bags in the room and hurried back downstairs for our first formation. It was there that I met Paul Brown and Randy Simon.

Paul was Ukrainian, a portly fellow recruited for football as a lineman. He was six foot six and intimidating. That is, until he spoke to you with a reassuring smile that suggested he was going to be a sincere friend with the best of intentions. Randy had a Korean mother and a father who had been in the Army when Randy was a kid. His father had died when Randy was growing up, perhaps explaining the dichotomy of Randy's maturity and childlike behavior. Randy was slightly shorter than I was and talked faster than anyone I had ever met. As I would learn, the majority of his antics were devoted to making everyone laugh.

The three of us stood together and whispered to each other, although we were supposed to be quiet and study our "smart" books. These "smart" books consisted of random basic cadet candidate knowledge. We were supposed to learn them and commit them to rote memory.

Our tactical officer and NCO were randomly choosing leaders, while the rest of us milled around in formation. Paul, Randy, and I continued to talk about where we were from and what we had done before.

The new CCs spent the rest of the week sizing each other up through sports or academics. It was disheartening when I heard that people were there to be quarterback or play basketball, and that they already had a high enough GPA from high school that they could have attended the Academy, but chose instead to come to USMAPS to better prepare themselves for the rigors of West Point academics. I wasn't sure if anyone else had gone through the same experience I had, but I wasn't going to let anyone know my scores unless absolutely necessary. Although I felt a certain level of comfort around my peers, my insecurities about my intelligence level were heightened. The mental game of "you vs. you" had begun very early even as I was just getting settled in at the Prep School.

One of the greatest things about the Army is that, regardless of where you stand in training or what the situation is, everyone struggles with their own life issues. Some of us deal with leaving their girlfriends, some want to be with their families, and others are afraid of the unknowns in life. The first night I met my roommate, I realized that there are some people who fit in all three categories.

. . .

Rob Stoffel, my roommate, came from Riverside, California, and immediately became one of my good friends at the Prep School. Rob fit the prototypical mold of the "Surfer Dude" from California. He was of average height and weight with beach blonde hair. His carefree attitude, but eagerness to achieve greatness, suited well with me, and that agreement led to us being great roommates.

Rob was one of five quarterbacks trying out for the football team. He wasn't sure if football was what he wanted to do at the Academy, but he knew he wanted to be an officer in the Army. Rob was always willing to learn about the Army and constantly asked me questions about my life before the Prep School. We spent the better part of the first night laughing and talking about things that happened in our former lives. I had learned in the Army that having a quality roommate made any situation better, regardless of the difficulty. I could tell that our friendship was going to last for years. Rob had his girlfriend's framed picture on his desk. I couldn't afford any distractions from my studies, so I refused to put up pictures of any girls, friends, or family. I had to focus on academics, which was already my worst enemy.

During the first three weeks of Prep School, everyone attended the Cadet Candidate Orientation (CCO). It was run by reserve drill sergeants who proved to be much nicer than the regular Army drill sergeants I had encountered while in basic training and AIT. They understood that we were there for academics and sports, and not so much for the military side of preparation. (Later, years after my experience, the military portion of the CCO was extended to four weeks with the addition of an eight-day field training exercise (FTX) that culminates with M-16 familiarization, land navigation, and obstacle courses.)

Sgt. First Class Sutton oversaw various classes in the mornings that ranged from learning how to do laundry to shining boots and ironing uniforms. The drill sergeants would then drill us in Drill and Ceremony (D&C) in the afternoons. D&C was the only military skill we would learn during CCO. At the end of CCO, all three companies competed in a D&C competition. Beneath a burning Jersey sun, approximately fifty CCs from Alpha Company (my company) stepped onto the parade ground, sweating, while humming the popular tune "Stand By Me" and performing marching movements. Even to this day, when I hear the voice of Ben E. King my body instinctively goes to parade rest. We managed a second-place finish in the competition, but marching was about the last of my concerns as I felt that the academic school year was quickly approaching.

At the end of the first week we had our first room inspection, which was to set the standard for the rest of the academic school year. Rob and I spent many hours getting our room ready. We wiped down every flat surface and made sure that our beds were so tight that quarters would bounce off them. We did everything according to Sgt. First Class Sutton's "standard" so we wouldn't have to deal with his wrath.

The inspection began on a Saturday morning, and we initially thought that being at the end of the hallway was the prime location. However, the drill sergeants and Sgt. First Class Sutton began their inspection in the room next to us—where Paul was living—which meant that ours was the second room to be checked.

As we stood at parade rest, and they checked the first room, we heard them yelling about standards. Several items hit the wall. Rob and I looked at each other and shared one thought: maybe we will do better at next week's inspection.

After ten minutes of the Sergeant scrutinizing the room next to us and belittling Paul's existence, it was our turn. Sweat dripped off our brows. Any person in his right mind would be nervous, but our hard work had already determined our fate for us that day.

Sgt. First Class Sutton stormed into our room and looked at our pairs of low quarters and boots and realized how shiny they were.

"Who's the IR?"

"IR" was only one of the place's many abbreviations, and stood for invitational reservist, which was the official way of saying "civilian."

I answered the question. "Cadet Candidate Stoffel, Sergeant."

"That's what I'm talking about," he yelled out into the hallway. "THAT'S WHAT I'M TALKING ABOUT!"

Sgt. First Class Sutton's excitement ran through our veins and showed that he believed we were the kind of CCs that would make it through both here and West Point because we were unselfish and willing to help each other. He told us that the phrase "cooperate and graduate" should constantly be on our minds. He left and explained to the rest of the company that he wasn't even going to check our room for the rest of CCO because he knew we were going to do the right thing.

As Rob and I began to snicker and high-five each other, one of the drill sergeants entered the room. Our eyes widened with fright. He admitted, however, that he was proud of us. Until then, I had never known there to be positive reinforcement in the Army. I still remember how that moment made me feel. I remembered it and applied it at every leadership opportunity possible.

Teamwork was an emphasis that had not been introduced yet, but obviously it was a key factor to success not only at the Prep School but in the Army as well. Rob and I found teamwork to be a natural thing and that was a big advantage for us. "Cooperate and graduate" is a common phrase used in higher education and military training schools. All it really means is to focus on the teamwork and everything else will take care of itself. In business, we have all had those great team players, haven't we? They sacrifice themselves for the team because it yields a greater result and that is what is important to them. I love working with, for, and around those people in any organization. How easy is it to spot someone who isn't that person? You know who I mean: the person who steals ideas to further their own gain, or talks poorly about you behind your back, or even sabotages your work to make themselves look better in front of superiors. Tread lightly with these people. Not everyone is skilled at identifying these peoples' true intentions within an organization and here's the thing: every organization, unit, and group has them. So be aware.

I would later learn that I did not have those clean-room

standards completely figured out. During my plebe year at the Academy, my roommates and I spent three weeks at the highest level of inspection known as SAMI (Saturday Morning Inspection). We were chastised for our lack of standards during this three-week punishment. I was repeatedly told that my roommates and I were going to get our "platoons killed" because of our lack of attention to detail. This decimation of our units would inevitably come from the fact that we would have a smudge on our tumblers in the medicine cabinet. These "details" were paid more attention at West Point than at any other stop I made in the Army, and for good reason. Minor details in pre-combat checks or inspections can mean life or death in a high-risk situation. While you are in a comparatively cozy academic environment, however, it's a difficult concept to grasp.

If everything at the Prep School had come as easily as that first room inspection, I wouldn't have anything to write about, nor would I have learned the most important lessons of my life in those ten months. Resiliency is the backbone of success. Difficulty and challenges come up constantly in our lives, and it's how we bounce back from each one of those and move forward that makes us stronger. When I am in any challenging situation, I may not always be perfect, but with age and experience, I have learned that the situation can't last forever. I knew that with USMAPS, if I kept pushing forward—regardless of the difficulty involved—it would have to eventually end.

After several Drill and Ceremony competitions and sessions in which our tactical officers and NCOs taught us about the Army, we were eager to begin the academic year. Or maybe I should say "they" were eager. If 99 percent of the students were ready for classes to start, I was part of the other 1 percent. I knew if I was going to hit a brick wall at Prep School, it was going to be in the classroom.

The day before academic classes began we all gathered in an auditorium, and the Commandant of the school began a speech about our class being the advanced guard for the bicentennial class of West Point—the "Golden Children," as later we were infamously known at the Academy. His candid speech gave me great hope for my future. He inspired us all with a clip from the movie *Glory*. As we watched it, we understood that there was more to battle than being tired or being scared. There was character and strength of heart. How could I know these words would ring so true for the academic battle that was about to begin? I still wasn't sure I was up to that challenge.

The Commandant showed the demographics of the Prepster class by SAT scores. Unfortunately, he showed the math portion first. All I could do was lower my head in shame as the curve was ruined by one dot on the lower left side. I had scored 310 out of 800 on the math portion of the SATs, and everyone in the auditorium knew someone in that room represented that dot. My newly acquired friends, Randy Simon, Eddie Johnson, and Paul Brown, all identified the dot and hurled out some insults about that guy. I wholly agreed with them. "Yeah," I said, "what an idiot!" I laughed on the outside, but deep down I began to hurt. I had never dealt well with humiliation. My older brother caused me to hate being made fun of, and now I had to make fun of myself in order to avoid any suspicion that I was "the dot."

Anyone who looked closely at me could identify the anguish beginning to build in my eyes. After an eternity, the next slide of the presentation flashed up. Expecting a moment of relief, I looked at the screen, but this slide showed the verbal score of the SATs. Yes, I represented the dot at the bottom left corner once again. I wanted to scream at the top of my lungs, go running out of the auditorium without looking back, and never be made fun of again about how stupid I was. I had scored 440 out of 800 on the verbal portion of the test, yet everyone else in the school had managed a score of 500 or higher. Not only was I 200 points lower than the lowest student on the math test, I was also 60 points lower than the lowest student on the verbal. Then Randy belted out a question, "What if that was the same guy as the math one?"

Based on my experience as an enlisted soldier, and even as an officer in charge of men in combat, I would argue that humiliation is a leader's best friend. The fear of embarrassment keeps leaders sharp in their day-to-day affairs. There aren't any superiors in the Army today who enjoy being proved wrong by subordinates.

Even today, when I'm humiliated, I hear that day's laughter echoing in my mind. With a painful laugh, I joined in, but all I wanted to do was disappear. However, the pain of that briefing taught me that I was never the person to sit back and let things happen to me.

I'm not sure how you feel when you are humiliated, but being humiliated tends to make me extremely frustrated initially, no matter if it is my peers, seniors, or subordinates making me feel that way. However, once I have had some time to process the action, I am hit with motivation to accomplish anything I set out to do. During that initial dip, humiliation is not always easy to shake, especially if it happens to come from the people we love most. I take that humiliation (really, pain) and I use it to push myself; every time I felt like I didn't belong at Prep School (which happened a lot), every time I got tired of studying, and every time I have wanted to quit anything in life, I have thought of that pain and I have pushed myself harder.

"I'll show them," I said to myself as we left the auditorium. "I will make it through this school and someone, somewhere, will need me someday."

Until that point, my educational background was not very good.

I went to a decent public high school, but I was a basketball player, and most people know that grades will be "given" to those who do well in high school sports. That was great at the time, but I wish my teachers had never done that. Now I was about to learn a valuable lesson at the Prep School. I never took college preparatory classes in high school, nor did I take any math classes that were not required. Furthermore, in my math classes my friends and I had stolen the teacher's edition book, made copies of the answers in the back, and turned those in for grades on a daily basis. We did this all the time in every math class required for graduation.

Every night I just copied the answers and never looked at how to actually do the math. How did I pass the tests? It wasn't that hard. I would skip class. Teachers would grade the tests, and the next day my friends would bring their graded copies to me. Yeah, I beat the system in high school, but it bit me in the ass in the end. I would later learn that when I reported to the Prep School, I was working with seventh-grade math abilities. As for all my other high school classes, they weren't much better.

My high school wasn't very demanding, and my main focus at that time was getting a basketball scholarship to get out of the state of Ohio. I knew I had a bigger life waiting outside of the small town of Owensville. The only thing that really distinguished the town was the county fair, which was held once a year. Despite the shortcomings of the town, I loved the environment there, and wouldn't trade the place where I grew up for anything. I had friends there, people I grew up with, who made the tiny village of Owensville worth living in. I enjoyed all of my years in the education system of Clermont Northeastern, and the teachers generally cared about the students. In high school, however, the kids get worse and the teachers' concerns seem to lessen. Now, I can see that this was a problem.

Although I liked having "easy teachers" when I was in high

school, I know now that my life at USMAPS would have gone much smoother if I had teachers who had cared enough to crack down on me and make me study. My pride in "beating the system" seems silly and unimportant today.

In a rural public high school, the priority isn't getting the students to college; the goal is often to simply get them out of the school without too many discipline problems. This I accomplished, and I moved on with my life. When I left high school, I felt ready for any challenge, but the Prep School's curriculum was not on my mind at the time of graduation. As the first day at the Prep School showed me, I would face a great deal of embarrassment because of my triumph of cheating in high school. Even to this day, with my nieces and nephews, I stress the importance of taking your education seriously from the start, rather than waiting to work hard on it. It is much more painful to learn seventh-grade math in college than it is in seventh grade. Trust me.

From a leader's perspective, you can't change the previous behavior of a person. You can only change the behavior of an individual once they are on your team. My actions in high school were detrimental to my future self. If I had had a mentor or coach lead me down the right path to success, I would have been much better off when I headed to the Prep School. As a leader, you are actually doing your subordinates a disservice if you don't challenge them to do things properly. A true leader never lets their team off easy, and can explain why making their life difficult is so important to their growth.

I didn't have long to wait for the humiliation to start. We all lined up in formation after breakfast and marched to the academic building where all classes were held. We had 210 students on the first day of CCO, yet now, for the first day of class, we had already dropped to 189. Although I felt a sense of accomplishment at having made it through the first few weeks of Prep School, the attrition was only beginning. Ultimately, we would graduate only fifty to sixty Prepsters from West Point from the class of 2002.

My first class was English. My teacher was a middle-aged, overweight man who loved to play the saxophone. I began to wonder if the instructors wanted to be here or if, like many of the students, they were just passing time until they got to something else. Whatever this teacher's intentions, he helped all of us ease into the academic world and calmed down many of us. He made himself approachable, and if we needed help with any of our essays or homework assignments, we could always go to him. I felt comfortable in the classroom, so comfortable that I decided my upcoming math class wouldn't be so bad after all. I was wrong.

I stepped into my math classroom with almost a feeling of arrogance. If I could conquer English, I could knock down math without a problem. My teacher, a small woman named Capt. Sharkey, entered the room and took attendance. As soon I saw her, I felt a rush of anxiety, as if I were about to face the Grim Reaper himself. After roll call, she went straight into her first day's lesson and didn't stop for forty-five minutes. For each of those forty-five minutes, I watched her whittle with ease at the equations and numbers on the board. I looked around; the class nodded with acceptance.

I could have sworn the class was in Latin or Chinese (which I would later take at the Academy). Those scribbles couldn't be math equations. Furthermore, where was the Captain coming up with these mythical numbers? I had concluded that she was going to end the class with a "just kidding," and the real class would begin any moment. She finished writing on the board, turned to the class and said, "Any questions?"

I had been told many times that there are no stupid questions, but apparently I had dove into the barrel of stupidity and pulled out a winner: "I don't understand, ma'am."

She laughed as if she didn't believe me. "What don't you understand?"

"Everything on the board," I said. "Can we first start with that big check thing with the numbers in it?"

She pointed at the square root symbol. "This thing?"

"Yes," I said, "that thing. What does that do?"

Before she could answer, the class exploded into laughter. Not a normal kind of laughter, either. There was some finger pointing, and some jackass even fell out of his chair at what apparently was the funniest question of the year.

Capt. Sharkey then proceeded to tell me that I was a "hopeless" student and that she wasn't even going to bother trying to teach me anything.

"I am not going to waste any of my time on you," she said. "I have to focus on the majority of the class that is going to pass." Her words hit home like nothing I had ever experienced before. In a matter of seconds, I felt all emotions—anger, humiliation, fear, rejection, and worst of all, hopelessness.

My confidence was shaken. Anger, though, was my first emotion. I thought about strangling her to avenge the humiliation she had caused me. Perhaps, however, she was doing me a bigger favor than I could imagine. It's possible she was trying to motivate me, but I don't think that was the case. Her stinging words clearly indicated that I was a student she wasn't going to help. She knew I was the dot on the left, and now the whole class did as well.

This wasn't the first time I had been told I couldn't do something. I had been told by my basketball coaches in high school that I would never get a scholarship. I had been told that I would never even get into the Prep School. I wasn't about to let this instructor rattle me with her tough girl captain act. I decided right then that I needed help and would do anything to survive.

Back in my room, I sat at my desk, my head in my hands. I was embarrassed to the fullest extent, and I wasn't sure what to do or how to act.

I went to Rob with my problems. We were in different math classes, but I didn't want to quit on the first day. I knew that my math class was a big bump in the road. I was afraid that I couldn't bring myself back to the reality of working hard enough to not only survive, but also to somehow excel here. I had never been a person who had accepted mediocrity, and I wasn't going to start now. I had worked harder than anyone else just to get here, and failure wasn't an option. I decided making the dean's list was the academic goal for the year. I wanted to get to that point, but I only hoped I didn't have to give the square root of a number to get there.

Despite my shortcomings in math, I knew there was only one thing that could bring me to the truth, one thing that could give me back my confidence. I was glad my first day of academics had ended, because basketball tryouts were about to start. In the gym, I knew I would be in my element.

three
·LOSING IN ALL ASPECTS·

. . .

"Courage is going from failure to failure without losing enthusiasm."

- WINSTON CHURCHILL

As I mentioned, one of the main reasons I attended the Prep School was to play basketball. I hadn't been sure at the time how the program worked with recruits and walk-ons. I learned soon enough that there were five recruits for the team and those five were going to play. Understanding this early didn't stop me from wanting to work toward my dream of playing college basketball at West Point, however, so I continued to battle through tryouts, just as I did my first day of classes.

John Pike coached the Prep School team. He could best be described as a motivator who turned small talent into big teams. Coach Pike was five feet seven, of stocky build, and balding. His Napoleon complex clearly served as motivation for his daily punishment of us. His colorful language wouldn't fully come out until tryouts were over and the team had been selected. By the end of the season, our team regularly answered to the phrase "fucking douchebags" without hesitation. Despite his raunchy language, every person on that team admired and respected Coach Pike. He represented everything that you love about coaches. He cared about his players with an unconditional love that a true father exemplifies in great times and in bad. To this day, I think of his techniques and his ability to motivate the team and how grateful I am for getting to have him as a coach.

We also had a graduate assistant, 2nd Lt. Chris Springer, who turned out to be the good cop of the two personalities. He fit the mold of a typical West Pointer. He had rugged good looks at six feet three with brown hair and blue eyes. The female CCs would swoon at his arrival. His soft-spoken manner was the exact opposite of Coach Pike. He was a graduate fresh out of West Point selected by Coach Pike to help train the team for the season. As Coach Pike tortured us with suicide drills, 2nd Lt. Springer winced at each painful lap we finished.

The first day of tryouts reminded me of the scene in the movie *Hoosiers* when the coach played by Gene Hackman wants to determine what kind of hand he has been dealt during his first practice with his new team. As I looked around at the other players, I started to realize that I was the two of clubs in a hand of aces and kings. As I was getting sized up by the coaching staff, I started remembering all the times when I had played pick-up ball. I would be chosen last because of my height and, unfortunately, my color.

I looked back on my basketball career and its start in the sixth grade. It was just a hobby to fill my time between the football and baseball seasons. A friend of mine suggested that I play with him and there were only six guys on the team. After trying wrestling and being made into a pretzel in several different fashions, I reluctantly showed up without a uniform for the first basketball game. My friend's father, Art Bass, coached the team. Although I didn't know who Bobby Knight was at the time, Coach Bass had the same attitude as Coach Knight. His raspy voice and height were enough to scare a room full of sixth graders. Before the game started, he showed me a few simple moves. He looked at the other two guys who were just filling spots, and he told me I was starting. Within minutes I was hooked. This game, I thought, required no talent to be on the starting team. Yeah, this was the sport for me.

Or maybe it did require a bit of athleticism. We only won one game that season, but I found a love for a sport that would surpass all other sports. I played the entire season and scored a total of eight points, all in one game. I lost my glasses during that game, and that most likely was the key to my sudden shooting accuracy.

Another year passed, and it was basketball season again. The coach we had was so large he couldn't even bring both of his hands together to shoot the ball. He was our science teacher, and seemed like a candidate for heart bypass surgery at any time. He looked like a science teacher, not a basketball coach. But he was our coach, and in seventh grade you give your coach respect. At least when he's watching. When he's not, you make fun of him at every chance. I was a starting player the entire season, and it was great. Once, we won a triple-overtime game with only four players left on the court. In my eyes, that remarkable game would go down as one of the best in seventh-grade history. To anyone else in the school it meant nothing. The way memory serves us in relation to sports is remarkable. We always remember being the heroes, never falling short and being the goat. Despite those victories, we ultimately learn the most from our losses, both in basketball and life. Sports had become my measure of resilience, which I needed for many things later in life.

My eighth-grade season was a disappointment. I found myself sitting on the bench through every game unless we were losing by a ton and there wasn't much time left. I might have also made it onto the floor if we were ever winning by a ton, but that situation never arose.

I finally found myself in one game in the middle of the season. My father had driven quite a distance to watch the game, and I wasn't going to disappoint him if I got the chance to play. The coach put me in during the third quarter, when we were down by more than twenty-five points. Surprised, I hustled to the scorer's table to check in. I was angry because the coach wouldn't let us play unless it was in this type of situation. For all the other players who sat the bench, I decided to provide a moment the crowd would never forget.

I went in during a free throw, and we got the ball back after the other team made the shot. I received the inbounds pass to bring the ball down the court, but the kid guarding me stole the ball and headed for the other basket. With my pent-up aggression at an all-time high, I waited until he leapt for a lay-up and then pushed him so hard that he flew into the mats underneath the basket.

He was knocked unconscious. The crowd reacted. The boy's parents began screaming at me and came out on the court. The coach was screaming at me, and he came out on the court. The referees were screaming at me, and they were already on the court. All I could do was smile. The referees immediately kicked me out of the game, and I went straight to the locker room and grabbed my gear. My smile was a façade. It wasn't meant to be malicious, just an indicator that I was unhappy with my performance and my place on the team and in life.

Have you ever felt that way? Put on a smile for the world to see while deep down you have many emotions that you are afraid to share with anyone? Many of us do that today, partly because we don't all have outlets to share those emotions. In a world where social media suggests that life is great all the time, we all know that isn't possible. We have things that get us down sometimes, and it's okay to share that with those around us.

The coach didn't want me to ride on the bus with the rest of the players because of my attitude problem, so my dad agreed to drive me home. I thought I was giving some justice to a team that was killing us, but the coach never looked at it in that manner. After I knocked the other player down, I wasn't angry anymore, so I wasn't sure what sort of anger management problem I had.

As my father and I walked down the hallway of the school, he looked at me and grinned. I imagined he was reviewing an instant replay of the moment on the court in his mind. I couldn't believe I had just blown my first chance to play early in a game by nearly killing a kid. He gave me the fatherly nod of approval, like the one when a father finds out that his son beat the bully up at school. Approval always won over any embarrassment that might have taken place. I kept my silence, and we headed home without exchanging many words. I had proven a point to my coach. I thought it was loyalty to the team, but in reality it made me look uncoachable. All I wanted to do was play, but now I knew that I wasn't going to get off the bench for the rest of the season. It didn't matter anyway, considering I would have only have been in for a maximum of sixty or so seconds in the remaining six games.

One day after the season, the coach pulled me aside. He let the rest of the students leave and sat me down to explain my "future" in basketball.

"David," he said, "you're a smart boy. You should try something other than basketball."

"I love basketball," I replied with a sorrowful glance. "I want to keep playing and be on the varsity team so I can play on Friday nights." The mere idea of playing varsity sent adrenaline surging through my veins.

He shook his head. "Son, you won't ever play on a Friday night. Those players are great, and you struggled to make your eighth-grade team."

I stormed out of the classroom with tears in my eyes. No one had ever told me I couldn't accomplish something before. What I didn't know at the time was that I would hear the same defeatist attitude again many times.

We all face these people in life. The sad thing is that most of us quit when we have a respected authority in our life tell us that we aren't good at something. In a world where most of us need instant gratification, we can't possibly think about the years it takes to master something. We only become great at something once we make the decision to not look back and realize it's a game of incremental success, not great strides. Whatever you choose to be great at or whatever dream or goal that you are trying to pursue, the only ones who become successful at it are the ones who just don't give up. Especially when someone close to us tells us to give up on it. That's when it can be the hardest.

I wanted to show the coach that he didn't know me and the sacrifice I was willing to make to play basketball. I wanted to show him that he was wrong and that I was better than he thought I was. I only had one problem: at the moment, he was right. I wasn't sure how I was going to fix my basketball inabilities. That year, I became quite adept at skipping school. I mastered the art of turning up my waterbed—yes, I had a waterbed at the time—and I would lie my head on the heater portion to get a good hot forehead going. Everyone knows that mothers love to measure a fever with a hand to the forehead. I skipped twenty days of school that second semester of eighth grade, and then I saw the movie that changed my life.

I know some people will say that a movie doesn't have the ability to change a person's life, but at such an impressionable young age, I was going to be on my way with a new positive attitude toward school and basketball. I watched the movie *Pistol Pete: Birth of a Legend* and immediately wanted to emulate Pete Maravich. In the movie, he is an eighth-grader who makes the varsity team and leads them to the state high school championship. I thought that if he could do it, surely I could to do it by my ninth grade year. I guess I was naïve, but sometimes the people who have the least knowledge about something work the hardest.

This is where analysis paralysis kicks in for most of us in life. As we gain more experience, get smarter, get older, we begin to rationalize to ourselves that we can't accomplish something because of too many roadblocks. In certain events in life, it's better just to put your head down and work. And work. And work. Until that thing becomes a reality. Don't count how many hours it will take to get there, just know that "there" comes with hard work and time— but you have to give it the time.

My life had changed, and therefore I changed my attitude about attending school. If I didn't attend school, I wasn't allowed to play basketball. After watching the movie, I had perfect attendance for the rest of the semester. I began to drill on my own, practicing three-pointers and free throws in particular. I even played one-on-one against my brother. Despite my brother being a wrestler, he was always a hundred pounds heavier and a foot taller than I was until my sophomore year of high school. His physical prowess was daunting. He beat me every game in those days, yet I persevered to get better. I practiced all summer long. I became determined that if I was going to pick one sport to play in high school, it was going to be basketball. I had no choice. I had to prove the naysayers wrong.

I spent countless hours every day honing my skills in order to make the varsity team and to lead my school to a high school championship, just as my new idol Pistol Pete had done. I figured I would earn my popularity that way. I was wrong in more ways than one.

The fall finally came. It was my freshman year, and tryouts didn't exactly go as planned. Still, I thought surely they would at least allow me on the junior varsity team. But I had been sent all the way down to our freshman team. It wasn't so bad, I thought. I had been on the same team with these guys the year before, and I knew all my practice would pay off.

I sat the entire year without any ten-second payoffs for working hard in practice. I was horrible, as was made clear by my lack of playing time. The coach played his five starters, one of whom was his son, for the whole game, every game, and I wasn't going to get the chance to even throw someone into the mats this season. Not only was I not playing, but I was depressed because basketball had become my life, and I was atrocious at it. My brother's success in all his sports didn't help my situation. He was a great athlete. My sister was naturally smart throughout her entire time in high school. To make matters worse, they were both popular in their classes. I made myself out to be a loser in my mind, and I wasn't sure how to not be one.

I wanted to be great at basketball. I just didn't know how. I felt depressed for the majority of my freshman year because I wasn't as successful as my brother and sister. I realize now that I wasn't the only one. A lucky few fit right into the elite crowds of popularity and success. My brother and sister had both been able to accomplish that feat in their freshman years, and I began to wonder what was wrong with me.

I look back now and understand that the majority of teenagers feel insecure about themselves. The changing voices, the inability to grow hair in the right places, puberty. I think we sometimes forget how hard it is to be a teenager and what a bitch it was just to be yourself. I think we all wanted to be popular at the age, didn't we? It takes many years to learn that popularity and fame aren't what they are all cracked up to be. It's ironic that I see people today (adults and teenagers) try so hard to be unlike everybody else, but instead, all of that effort to be different makes them look like they conform to the majority. Just being yourself—your values, beliefs and being your best—is admirable, and that is enough.

But it wasn't long before I encountered someone who was ready to bet against me. My freshman coach sat me down and told me that basketball wasn't the path I should choose and that I should focus more on academics. I largely discredited his opinion since he allowed his son to start on the team for the entire season, but I also struggled with the reality of what he said. He was right, but I still wanted to prove him wrong. At that time, in the early 1990s, Michael Jordan was at the peak of his career, and his story of getting cut from the varsity team his sophomore year was widely known. I had the utmost respect for a player of his caliber. He inspired me. His story stuck with me as I began another summer of training for basketball. I vowed that I wasn't going to be Michael Jordan and not make varsity as a sophomore. I would do better than that. I was willing to do whatever it took to get there.

I started with the basics and trained on everything from dribbling to passing. My practice time spanned ten to twelve hours a day. I played so much basketball that I dreamed of it every night. I practiced dribbling so much that my hands bled. At any given time during the summer, I had a minimum of two band-aids on my fingers.

Let me explain something here. I LOVE the process of working toward making a dream a reality. As I found out later in life, one of my top three strengths is focus. I have the ability to work on something for hours without break or consideration for other things, especially if I'm passionate about it. When you give yourself wholeheartedly to your passion, there is no greater feeling in the world than that. For me, it is the underlying theme to becoming successful. Never quit on something that you are passionate about. Your passions may change over time (I know mine have), but that same fervor and zest must always stay the same.

My dedication to basketball had begun with the dream of

making varsity as a freshman, but I was determined now to get a basketball scholarship to play in college. If I could only make the team, that would be the foot in the door I needed.

Fall tryouts of my sophomore season began, and I realized that the coaches placed me on the junior varsity every time we lined up for scrimmages. I kept playing well throughout the open practices we had, but potential doesn't land you a position on the varsity team when the junior varsity team still needs players.

I had made a life-sacrificing decision to put everything into basketball, and I watched my chance disappear with every practice as I slipped down to the JV team. The idea of getting cut from varsity ripped at my soul, and yet all I could do was stare down at the other end of the court where the varsity guys practiced. I was disheartened by the decision, but I continued to grow and become better with each game.

The head coach of the varsity team recognized my potential, but decided it was best for me to wait until the next year to play for him. He later admitted to me that his decision to cut me was the biggest mistake of his coaching career. I would happily agree with him then. However, it didn't help me when I was a sophomore in high school with a self-esteem problem.

I led the JV team in scoring, assists, and steals. I was so blind to the fact that I was on the right track. All I could focus on was not being on the varsity team, and I neglected to celebrate the small victories. As a leader in any organization, failure to celebrate leads to lower engagement of employees in the long run. People want to know that what they do matters. Giving yourself that kind of credit is difficult as well, but without having gratitude for the small victories, we can all become easily disenchanted with life—so make sure that there is a place in your life for being thankful and enjoying the small wins.

Even so, I felt I had wasted another year. I tried to look at it positively, however, and soon realized that the more playing time I got on the JV team, the more experience I gained. Logically, that made sense, but it was difficult to reason with a kid with dreams as big as mine. I continued with my big dream of playing college basketball and started the next summer more determined than ever.

Again, I continued to polish my skills. I played at different parks across the city and proved myself against the most difficult players who had started on their varsity teams the year before. I began to make a name for myself on several different playgrounds, and, for the first time since I began this journey, I felt confident. One day at a park in a neighboring town of Batavia, I played one-on-one with one of the most respected players in the area. At first, his quickness allowed him to move freely around the court. However, he couldn't contend with my outside shooting. Against each other, with no one else watching, we went to war. With the game point on the line, I had the ball. The only thought that crossed my mind was, "If I beat him that will mean everything to me. If he wins, no one will care." I drained the three-pointer in his face as I faded away from the basket. I never told anyone about my victory over the playground king because, mentally, I had already become the best player I could for the next season.

I only had to convince one more person that I deserved to be a starter, and the coach was going to see a whole new player.

Fall tryouts for my junior year began. I was on the second team of the varsity now. The coach was starting seniors over me, and I was extremely bothered by it. I approached him about it, but the only advice he gave was that I should have worked harder over the summer. I couldn't believe what I'd heard considering I was confident I was the best player on the team and that everyone knew it except for the coach. Plus, I was sure no one had worked harder than I had.

As we prepared for the first game of the season, the coach announced that he had suspended four seniors for partying the night before a scrimmage. I was so excited. The night before the game, I couldn't sleep. I was starting on the varsity team for the first time in my life. I was a nervous wreck.

The next night, the coach got us prepared for warm-ups, and as soon as I hit the court and the game began, I didn't hear anyone except the coaches and my teammates. I didn't feel winded when I sprinted, and I moved my feet on defense better than I had in any practice. I needed to keep this starting position, and I started the season in an unstoppable zone.

I hit every shot I took and finished the game with twenty-four points. Every three-pointer felt easy. I stole the ball five times and had eight assists. I even rebounded the ball six times as the point guard. I had the best game our coach had seen from a point guard since he had started his career. Needless to say, I started for the rest of the season and the rest of my career in high school.

I earned first-team all-conference both years, all-city both years, and all-district both years. I had worked hard and daydreamed my way into a starting position on the team, and it had paid off. Although I had achieved much more than I had originally wanted, I was yearning for something more and didn't know it. I did recognize that all those hours practicing at my house had turned into these accolades and that was something I had never experienced before. I felt satisfied with the way that things turned out, but I kept having this feeling that there was something more for my life than just basketball. I couldn't put my finger on it.

All I had left to do was somehow get a basketball scholarship as a five feet ten slow guy from the country. That proved to be a little more challenging than I had originally thought.

I sent my stats to every college in the tristate area of Ohio, Kentucky, and Indiana, and not one school sent anything back to me. I was crushed because I knew I had potential to be great if a school would only give me the chance. I still didn't have a scholarship by April of my senior year, so I joined the Army Reserves as what seemed like my only opportunity to get out of Owensville. The irony is that the weekend after I joined the military, I played a tournament in Louisville, Kentucky. I had scouts from junior colleges all over me. Five schools offered me scholarships as soon as they saw me play. I quickly made a decision to attend Jacksonville Bible College without even looking at the school or knowing much about the coaching program there. Jacksonville is in Texas and participates in one of the most demanding junior college conferences in the nation, and that was all I needed to know.

I was excited at the idea of playing with the best in the nation at a junior college. However, I still had to attend two months of basic training before I started the fall semester. Without touching a basketball for that length of time, my skills got rusty. The coach at Jacksonville immediately decided to put me on redshirt status, so I quit the team. After a month, I decided my dream would never come true, so I packed up my things and left. This was one of the hardest decisions I have ever made. It wasn't just a basketball decision either. I sat in some classes, and I just wasn't getting that part of school either. I felt that I had done pretty well in basic training, and I really enjoyed the Army atmosphere—again, something I had never experienced before—and those were the driving factors for leaving. I felt that if basketball was supposed to be part of my life again, it would find a way.

Without really thinking about it, I knew my best decision was to go back to what I had enjoyed so far: the Army.

I went back into the Army and immediately started playing

basketball again in Pensacola, Florida, at my AIT. I played in the lunchtime basketball league and for the Army on two different posts. I had become a basketball player with the Army training school that I was attending. My confidence grew as I saw and played with many different styles of players.

Once I was accepted into the Prep School, I counted on my playing in all those different leagues to have prepared me for anything I was about to face. Anything, that is, except a coach who would only play his five recruits. Of course, I had seen this act before in my freshman year of high school. Seeing it again scared me. Back at my first day of tryouts, I was amazed to find that my basketball career was right back where it had started.

After a few days, it became apparent who had experience playing and who didn't. The coach made quite a few cuts from the team. We ended up with twelve players, five of them already recruited to West Point. We started practice early, and the first team started with those five recruits. That made it difficult for anyone to make a change in the program with the coach. Periodically, the coach would switch one of the starters with his counterpart to motivate one of the starting five, but it rarely worked because they knew they were locked into those positions.

I continued to work hard throughout the beginning of the season, but, despite my best efforts, the coach only played his five guys. I remembered my freshman year in high school and thought how unfair this was for the team.

This coach was a little different, however. When the decision was made on who played, he made it clear. Coach Pike was adamant that he was the boss and no one challenged his authority. I sat the first five games of the season with other fellow players who never got off the bench. One of the players, Joe Peppers, a friend of mine from Chicago, felt the same pain, and we exercised the theory that misery loves company. We sat at the end of the bench and did our sad, moping song.

"This is bullshit, Joe. We're better than those guys out on the court right now."

"I know, Dave. One day we'll get our chance, and he'll know that he made a mistake sitting us these first few games."

Despite our negative attitudes, we never gave up hope that someday we would play. It wasn't until the second quarter of the academic year that we would see real playing time, and until then Joe had to motivate the both of us, because I was struggling with every facet of the Prep School curriculum. It was during these times that I realized self-motivation is key to achieving goals. However, realizing that I wasn't always going to be motivated during difficult times is when I learned to lean on others.

Surrounding yourself by other amazing, supportive people is not an easy thing to do, but when you recognize those who support you unconditionally, you do everything it takes to keep them in your social circle.

four

·GOD AND SPAGHETTI·

. . .

"God helps those who help themselves."

- BENJAMIN FRANKLIN

My basketball career wasn't going well, and academically, I was drowning more than I actually knew. Even so, I had the motivation and drive to continue my studies. I had to start again at a seventh-grade math level, and the weeks of academics were quickly passing. I had to learn the daily material my instructor was teaching, fake that in order to pass, and then continue to study the remedial books I had bought on my own. I was in the same position I had been in at Jacksonville Bible College, and I was afraid of failing again.

I began a regimented schedule of studying math for eight to ten hours per day, even on the weekends. This felt very familiar to the way I had to become successful at basketball. Another member of the basketball team, Charles Woodruff, became my tutor, and, more importantly, my friend. Every day I amazed him with my lack of math abilities. Yet he continued to help me with every problem.

One day, as Charles was tutoring me, I looked at the calculator and told him not to laugh at me. "Chuck, what is this sin (I pronounced it like the word used in church to describe murder and stealing), cos, and tan?"

He couldn't help but laugh. "You're not serious," he said.

I stared at him without blinking, and he knew that I really didn't have a clue about the three buttons. "They stand for sinusoidal, cosine, and tangent. They are used for trig."

This floored me. "Do you think I will make it that far at this school?"

He patted me on the shoulder and gave me a boost of confidence. "You and me, we're going to make it through here and West Point, and there isn't going to be anyone who stops us." Charles's confidence in himself gave me strength.

As a leader, confidence is of the utmost importance. No one, and I mean no one, follows a person just because of rank or position. If all else is failing in the world around you, having confidence shows subordinates or team members that you have everything under control. Any self-doubt will be magnified and obviously visible to everyone around you.

I thanked Charles every chance I got for tutoring me and putting up with my stupid questions.

Charles continued to teach me daily with a positive attitude. He had prepared himself throughout high school to be in this position. Without him, I would have never made it through the Prep School. He was one of the many people throughout the year who helped me survive, and I was grateful to have him in my life, because he also talked to me about God.

I had a lot of support from friends and family at home, but with them so far away I wasn't certain that I would succeed. I had re-established my relationship with God, however, and it began to develop as I attended services on post every Sunday.

On my first Sunday at Prep School, I heard the most beautiful voice resonate throughout the church. It belonged to a special young lady in that day's attendance. I was amazed by her talent and kindness. Her name was Josie Holmon. Josie and I instantly became friends. She was in a different company, and after our first Sunday services, we spent hours talking to each other. I learned all about her. We had similar interests, and I decided that I needed something to help me stay interested in church. Choir would be the best way to keep me accountable. With her voice and my need for God, Josie and I both joined the choir and prayed together at the services.

I found that prayer became a necessity for me throughout the West Point process. I began to enjoy the prayers and the people in the choir. They were not the greatest singers in the parish. They were merely the people who were willing to embarrass themselves every Sunday in front of the parish. I was one of the few and willing, and thus I earned a spot with the choir members.

When Josie and I joined, I think we brought the average age of the members down from seventy-five to sixty-five, but it was fun hanging out with the older people in the surrounding community. They told us each week how proud they were of us and how much they supported what we were doing. To us, they seemed a lot like our grandparents, who we rarely had the opportunity to see.

Our choir leader was a kind woman who tolerated the poor singing and somehow allowed the members to substitute spirit for talent. Throughout the Prep School, I continued to pray and sing with the choir. I prayed every Sunday for God to give me a miracle and allow me to somehow make it through school. I had attended church and prayed for several things when I was younger, and I was always able to accomplish things that seemed impossible.

My first prayer for something big in my life had been for a basketball scholarship after high school. I attended a Catholic church all my life and completed the proper requirements such as baptism, first communion, and confession. In ninth grade I finally found my dream to pray for, and I continued to do that each night and every Sunday as I attended services. "Dear Lord," each prayer started, "thank you for everything you have given me, and all I ask is to be able to get a college scholarship." I prayed this daily before I went to sleep, and I always felt that God played a big role in my life. The miracle of getting a scholarship actually happened at the end of my senior year in high school. The next time I resorted to heavy prayers was during basic training.

There is a common phrase with prayer: we pray in our time, and God answers in His. Here's the funny thing, though: God doesn't always answer your prayers *on purpose*. It takes many years to find out why things don't happen the way we want them to. I had prayed for a college scholarship, but that wasn't where I was supposed to be. I had a greater calling than basketball—to be a leader in the U.S. Army—and it wasn't until many years later that I accepted that calling. Sure, I could have gone to another junior college or low-level school and played basketball, but that's not the way I see it now. Basketball was an instrument to teach me how to work hard and see results—that's why basketball was in my life— that's all.

My friend and I had joined the choir during basic training because we were allowed to leave our quarters earlier without drill sergeant supervision. We received this luxury in order to practice, and it was considered an honor that the drill sergeants trusted us enough to allow us to walk down the street without them yelling at us.

My prayers every Sunday consisted of simply wanting to make it through the hell of basic training. I always prayed for strength and courage to be able to meet any challenge. God listened to me once again and gave me little pushes whenever I thought I couldn't push myself anymore. I learned to trust in God, and when I went to AIT in Pensacola, I began my prayers for acceptance to the Prep School. I was relieved, but not shocked when I finally received my acceptance to the school, but I always gave God my respect, and He has always been a part of my life, even when I thought He wasn't.

While at the Prep School, I didn't feel that participating in the choir and attending church was going to be enough for the miracle I was asking for, so I made it mandatory to attend the Wednesday dinner prayers as well.

The Wednesday prayers included a home-cooked meal from people in the community. I am not sure if it was the spaghetti or the Lord that most attracted me to the meetings, but I decided that it was best that I had a little bit of both. I liked the idea of God and spaghetti together. These meetings helped me refocus my prayers on the task at hand and allowed me to make time to study the Bible. Up to that point, learning the math equations that had eluded me for so many years was taking priority over the Bible, so now I was trying to please everyone in my life.

The evenings began with everyone gathering together and holding hands with one another. As young men, we always found it funny to hold hands with each other. So even with the Commandant's wife as the group leader of the Wednesday night prayers, as prayers began, so did the tickling of hands. Juvenile as it was, each person tried to make the other laugh during prayer. Yes, it was disrespectful to the Commandant's wife, but it sure was amusing when it happened. I compared it to laughing in church when I was younger.

Brian, my brother, and I weren't forced to attend church when we were eight and nine years old. Instead, we were given a choice. We could either go inside the church or sit in the car. In the summer, with 95 percent humidity, church was the better option.

We always began the service with my sister on one side of my mother and Brian and me on the other. Any mother who has two sons knows this combination just doesn't work. Sure, we were respectful of the priest at the beginning. Once the kneeling and standing game started, however, we couldn't help messing with each other. My favorite trick was to sneak the hymnal onto the pew when Brian wasn't looking so he could get a nice surprise when he sat down. My brother's personal favorite was to elbow me off the kneeler when we were getting ready to bend down. These games never got old, but the best game of all was to fart silent farts and get the other to acknowledge it. This game usually continued for several minutes. Brian and I tried not to laugh. We both would be smiling, however, and Mom knew we were up to something. She'd give us a stern look and tell us to "cut it out." Usually this was enough for us to get our acts together, but not one memorable Sunday.

On that particular day, we were in the mood for a good laugh, and it eventually happened at my mother's expense. The fart game continued, and sure enough, one of mine turned out to be so loud that the priest stopped his sermon. Brian laughed out loud. My sister was embarrassed, but not by the farting. My mother slapped us both and dragged us out the side door of the church. She swatted us around and treated us like the hooligans that we were. My sister reluctantly followed us out. We were pushed into the car, and silence fell over our 1976 red and white Ford Pinto station wagon. On Sundays, the radio station played our favorite oldies, but my great Sunday's rendition of "Yakety Yak" wasn't going to be heard today. The radio remained off.

Mom continued to yell at us as we drove home. She said she couldn't believe our actions. We were eight and nine years old, and I'm not sure what kind of behavior she expected, but I thought it was pretty normal. By the time she regained her composure, we were almost home. Brian and I looked at each other and gave the thumbs up and spent the rest of the day in our rooms. My brother and I always felt as if we had small victories against my mom in those moments. We didn't know it, but it was the beginning of us being part of a team, together. My mother made us stay there to think about God and how we had offended the Lord that day. Now, during the Lord's Prayer back at the Prep School, my friend and I developed a laughing disorder similar to the one Brian and I had experienced. We constantly interrupted the group at the Prep School.

The Wednesday night dinners were so bountiful that we even had a few people fall asleep during the Bible study. The dinner could only be pasta and lasagna with salads on the side. Each week, we thanked the people who supported us and prayed for their families to make it back the next week with our favorite ziti. Some people came to the dinner and ate without ever going up to the Bible study, but I could never do that. The people who brought the food worked hours to feed us, and I always felt guilty if I didn't give a little time to God each week—a bit more, that is, than my daily prayers.

The Commandant's wife, however, didn't appreciate that Ryan Murphy and I would get the giggles during prayer time. As Ryan would say the words "Our Father," I always leaned toward his ear and whispered, "Hooah." This is an Army term that can be used as "yes," "no," "will comply," or anything that can shorten a sentence. Mostly, it's supposed to convey enthusiasm, an eagerness to get out there and destroy the enemy. Sure, we were enthusiastic about God, but in this case, the word's violent connotations didn't quite fit into our Bible study and prayers.

As I explained earlier, trying to not laugh in church is one of the hardest things a young person can do. Ryan would begin again, and again I would whisper softly. He would lose it. I would look at the Commandant's wife and shake my head with disgust. She told him one week that if he couldn't control himself, he shouldn't come back until he could. I enthusiastically agreed with her, although I was the main reason he was showing such a lack of concern for the prayers and Bible study. God was watching, but I'm sure He was laughing right along with me.

Throughout the year, Ryan and I met with the Commandant's wife and the rest of the regulars for the Wednesday night dinner, prayers, and Bible study. It was a necessary break that motivated me for the last two days of the workweek. We all need those mental breaks from our steepest challenges. Although making it through USMAPS and getting to the Academy was becoming an obsession, sometimes our best work comes from taking a step back and looking at things from a different perspective. My faith that God would help me through my difficult situations has never changed.

Am I a completely devout Christian? The answer is no. Have I believed in God since I was eight years old? Without a doubt. I thank God a lot these days—for everything I have. Gratitude, to me, is one of the biggest secrets to having a fulfilled life. Now, it doesn't have to be gratitude to my God. It could be gratitude to the world, to another God—to whatever you believe in—but giving thanks daily for all the things we have is a must to move forward. How can you have more things in your life if you aren't thankful for the things that you have now?

I continued with my practice of Sunday church in the choir and Wednesday Bible studies for the remainder of the year. I even finished my final step in Catholicism while at the Prep School.

I had never been confirmed when I was younger, but as my faith strengthened, I felt I was ready. I had my friend, Thomas Kilbride, serve as my sponsor for the ceremony. God was in my life, and I was thankful for His presence. I still attribute all of my successes in life to God, and making it through the Prep School was only the beginning of the long journey that shaped my life.

• PHOTOS •

Swearing in Ceremony on Day 1 at USMAPS

SFC Sutton barks an order at the Cadet Candidates

My USMAPS
yearbook photo

CPT Sharkey, my first quarter math instructor
at USMAPS

Charles "Woody" Woodruff,
my math tutor throughout
USMAPS

(From left to right) - Me, my brother, Brian, and my
father, George, at the Land Between the Lakes in 1999

1997-1998 Men's Basketball
team with Coaches John Pike
and 2LT Chris Springer

Major John Kirby, Director of Military
Training and the officer in charge of
the Men's Basketball Team

Taste of Heaven
(God and Spaghetti)

Listening intently in class

five

•ADDITIONAL INSTRUCTION•

...

"Tell me and I forget, teach me and I may remember, involve me and I learn."

- BENJAMIN FRANKLIN

The first quarter of the Prep School ended, and I had barely survived. The lowest grade a student can receive and still stay at the school is a 70 percent. I had earned 70 percent exactly. The class that had laughed at me was amazed to see me in their next quarter's classes. Thanks to Charles, I was able to study our current problems while reverting to my seventh-grade math level. Actually, I felt that in math, I was probably working at an eighth- or maybe ninth-grade level by the beginning of the second quarter. I was proud of myself for pushing along as well as I had, and the support from everyone around me had grown immensely.

At this time, the basketball season was in full swing. My study hours actually had increased because of the road trips involved. I would spend hours in the van with Charles, so he helped me study during our away trips.

We then started the second quarter of classes. My first day of math class, it became clear that Capt. Doniec, my new instructor, knew I was his weakest student, because he had me go to the board to complete a simple algebra problem. The problem was at least at the tenth-grade level, and I hadn't reached that point yet.

It wasn't enough to shame me in front of the class by choosing me to complete the problem, so he also had me sit down while he explained to the class why he wasn't going to recommend such a lazy student to West Point. I had never been described as lazy before, and this took me by surprise. Maybe it was a motivational tactic, but I just didn't get it.

I knew at this time that all recommendations came from our second-quarter instructors in order to make it to the admissions department in time. I was scared that he actually meant what he said, and what made it worse was that I felt better when the students were laughing at me. Needless to say, my humiliation was back and any amount of pride I had earned for myself had dissipated.

Humiliation can be our strongest teacher at a young age. No one likes to be embarrassed in front of peers—at any age. However, when we are younger, there is something that drives us, at least it did for me. Let me make a clear distinction here: there is humiliation and then there is getting laughed at by an entire class of the dots on the right. Being the dot on the left, my skin grew thicker because of the laughter. Don't feel sorry for me about the laughter. I believe it drove me to be a better student, person, and cadet candidate.

Capt. Doniec's comments burned in me and drove me to prove him wrong in every aspect. His comment that he had seen "lazy students" like me before contradicted everything I had done up until then. Yes, I had barely survived the first quarter, but that wasn't an indicator of the amount of effort I had put forth.

Math wasn't my favorite subject, but making people eat their words had become my favorite pastime. I had proven Col. Jones wrong when he had finally admitted me, I had shown myself to Capt. Sharkey, and I was going to add Capt. Doniec to the mixed company of people who had no faith in me.

I became more adept at completing problems without Charles's help by the middle of the second quarter. The equations and the problems started to make sense to me, and solving logic problems actually became fun.

I established a daily ritual of studying and playing basketball and got used to the fact that I was only going to get six hours of sleep a night until I could figure out all the problems assigned for homework. I awoke at six every morning, ate breakfast and studied until seven thirty, and went to classes. I studied between classes and before basketball practice. Then I came back after practice and went over that night's homework and completed as many of the logic problems and linear algebra problems as I could. These helped me understand everything I had missed in high school. Regardless of how hard I worked, by the end of the second quarter, I still didn't have a math teacher recommendation, and the SAT retake was coming up.

I've mentioned that I had earlier scored 310 out of 800 on the math portion of the SAT. To gain admission to West Point, I needed a better score. At the beginning of the school year, we received the SAT prep book so we could work through practice problems on our own time. I had done just that. Each day I did a minimum of two problems in preparation for the test.

I went to God for help with basketball and academics. I felt I had done everything possible to help myself survive mathematics.

In the second quarter, I met the single most interesting character at the Prep School: Dr. Matthew Ignoffo, my performance enhancement instructor. It was mandatory that every student take Dr. Ignoffo's class at some point during the year, and it was every Prep School student's nightmare. Dr. Ignoffo was a short, greasy-haired man who had acquired the wardrobe of a disco dancer from the seventies. His daily outfit consisted of really tight brown or brightly colored pants with a butterfly-collared shirt and a big gold chain that bounced as he walked. His raspy voice began every class with a "close your eyes" session. We would imagine ourselves at a peaceful state and prepare for the day's work.

Although Dr. Ignoffo scared me a bit, I went to him after class one day and asked if he could help. Once we began to talk about the problems I was having, he asked me about basketball. He had me write down on a 3" x 5" index card what I wanted to do with basketball and who I wanted to be. On one side of the card I wrote that I wanted to make every jump shot, and on the other side I wrote, "I am Michael Jordan." At first, this idea seemed weird to me because I knew both ideas were impossible. However, Dr. Ignoffo assured me that, although the ideas are impossible, I could still strive to reach my goals. Overall, the session only took half an hour. It gave me a new respect for him, because anyone who was willing to take time out of his schedule to help me was an important part of my learning process at the Prep School. This exercise helped me view Dr. Ignoffo in a different light. I don't believe I was fully ready for his techniques and his style at the time, but his help in building my self-confidence, especially after it had been torn down several times, was something I'll never forget as part of my great year at USMAPS.

Throughout my year at USMAPS, I heard Dr. Ignoffo horror stories. When people made negative comments in his class, for example, he would make them hold up their hands and shout, "I am a victim!" This was a technique to get a student to think positively about himself and his actions, but the way it came off sometimes made it seem as if he was attacking the person. No one escaped the Prep School without a Dr. Ignoffo story, and he made such an impression on the students that even years later, the mention of his name would cause any former Prepster to share an anecdote.

At the beginning of the year, we were instructed to save money for entrance to West Point. The minimum amount required for a cadet to enter school was $2,400. Each month, we had to show our TAC NCOs our savings account so he could compare it with the previous month's balance. Anyone who didn't save at least $240 from the last month was reprimanded, and if the action repeated, an allotment would be taken out of his or her paycheck and go directly into a savings account.

I entered the Prep School as a specialist with a pay grade of E-4. I made more than most people at the school, so I was able to save every month and have plenty left over for the weekends. In my ten months at the Prep School, I saved more than $10,000 in order to prepare myself for anything I wanted to do at the Academy. During the second quarter, I had already saved the $2,400 for West Point, and everything was starting to come together for me. Everything, that is, except the required recommendation from my instructor.

After months of struggling, I survived and passed once again. A B- means moving on, and I was extremely excited to not only survive, but do a little bit better that quarter. Despite Capt. Doniec's best efforts to keep me down, I overcame his insults and continued to work to the best of my ability. I was even more proud of myself this quarter, because I was able to complete over half the homework problems on my own, without Charles' help. I continued to study during Christmas break, and even tried to get ahead of the game by studying trigonometry on my own. I looked at the book for two weeks during break, however, and couldn't figure out a single trig problem. I knew I was going to be in trouble in the third quarter.

six

•GOAT WRESTLING•

. . .

"Youth is the gift of nature, but age is a work of art."

- STANISLAW JERZY LEC

I had finally reached the middle of the school year, and things were going well. I had passed the second quarter academically and had finally started a few games on the basketball team. I went home with confidence about my life at the Prep School.

My family had been proud of me every moment I was gone. I had called home so many times throughout the first semester to confess my thoughts of quitting. My dad often told me stories of my younger life and that always motivated me to continue at least another week. The problem in the early part of the year was that I failed so many tests and homework assignments that it didn't seem possible that I would get accepted to the Academy.

I stared at the ground and admitted to my father, "I can't do it, Dad. I can't make it." I said this nearly every week, and without a doubt, it struck a chord with my father. Dad would begin with his famous stories of my childhood, and I would find myself reminiscing. The goat story became his favorite. He was a truck driver, and he even told it to strangers he met on the road. If they ever met me, they would always identify me as the kid who wrestled the goat.

Dad's raspy, caring voice always began, "You were five years old. It was a gorgeous sunny day in the sizzling Ohio summer. Our next-door neighbors had a goat and a horse. The goat had somehow wandered over to our yard. I yelled at it for a few minutes, but it refused to leave and kept eating our grass. Brian came out with a bat. I told him to go and get that goat out of our yard. He left the yard screaming and ran back into the house. You came out right after that and asked me why he was so scared." Dad always grinned at this part of the story. "I told you to go get that goat out of the yard. You ran right over to that old goat, grabbed him by the head and wrestled him to the ground without thinking about it."

At the time, my father said, he didn't really think much about the significance of the episode; he definitely didn't see it as a moment that somehow defined my character. As I got older, however, the story weighed more on his mind, and he started to apply it to my life. He saw so many people in the world who are scared of the unknown, scared of their own dreams. People too scared to go out and chase their dreams, too scared of failure—those are the people whose dreams never come true.

"David, you never did anything in your life scared," he told me. "You did whatever it took to be successful, and I believe any problem you ever face in life will be just like that goat." He always made me feel better with the goat story because it had the feeling of one of Aesop's fables, complete with a valuable moral.

I, personally, have always loved this story. We have so many challenges in life, and here was mine at age five, a literal goat in the yard. Who are you when it comes to the goat in the yard? Do you take off running for safety or do you run right over to it and wrestle it to the ground? My father was right. I have always been someone who goes after it without much delay. I have been that way and will always be that way, but if you haven't always been someone who attacks a tough situation—how do you get to that point? Without hesitation. Don't think about the analysis of a situation sometimes, just run right over and grab the horns—then worry about what is going to happen next. Wait too long and that goat may head butt you. Hesitation in action is what keeps us in our nice, safe place in life. Running right over and taking it down—that takes us out of our comfort zone and ensures growth.

During my winter break, my family and I decided to take a road trip from Nashville, Tennessee, to Homestead, Florida. During basic training, my parents had moved from Owensville, Ohio, to Nashville because of my father's job as soon as I graduated from high school. Brian and I met at my parents' house in Nashville, and we started the trip—a seventeen-hour drive that would wear on everyone's patience. We took turns driving, however, and my mom and I ended up listening to music in the backseat.

A few months earlier, I had bought a CD by Boyz II Men. It had "Song for Mama" on it. As we were making our way through Georgia, I played it for her because she had always been there for me. She was always supportive and encouraged me to live my dreams. It was time to say thank you, and the song made it easier for me to express how I felt.

She cried for a long time, and then she hugged me and said, "David, I love you too." She had read my mind and knew what I was trying to say with a song. It made me feel good that we had bonded. Silence returned, and as I fell asleep watching the Georgia Mountains, I found myself doing math problems in my head, even in my dreams.

We stopped after ten hours in the car, climbing over each other in our rush to get out of the vehicle. We smelled from long hours of travel and couldn't wait to get cleaned up. Our first stop was Madison, Florida, where my aunt and uncle lived. Northern Florida wasn't what I expected. There were no beaches, just backwoods that would give the hills of Tennessee a run for their money. There was one bar at the end of my aunt and uncle's street. It also served as a general store, and it represented the entire business world of Pinetta, a township of Madison. The only thing that was fun about this place was the fact that the entire family had come to visit. Somehow, all thirty of us managed to squeeze into my aunt and uncle's double-wide trailer.

For the first few days we were bound to the trailer, and riding on three-wheelers became the only exciting daily event. I was twenty years old, as were my cousins. I couldn't think of anything to do, and we could only play so many James Bond video games on the Nintendo.

We spent Christmas Eve with the family in Madison, then headed to another aunt and uncle's place in Homestead. My family was excited about doing something new and seeing the better part of Florida. The drive was a little more than seven hours, and when we arrived, we were welcomed with fresh fish frying and a Christmas dinner. My Uncle Tim enjoyed frying fish that had just been caught, and my father always ate what was left over.

We spent a few days in Homestead, and my uncle took us out on his boat. Regardless of the time of year in Florida, it is always fun to fish in the ocean. We had a storied past of fishing on the Atlantic Ocean as a family. In fact, my father liked to tell one legendary story about a fishing trip from my early childhood. As with all good fishing stories, it was about the one that got away.

It happened on a salty day in the Atlantic when I was just five years old. It was my first fishing trip. We had caught small fish throughout the day. Then, in the late afternoon, I started to reel in what felt like the biggest catch of the year. I struggled with my pole, and my father wanted to help me.

"Back off!" I cried. "I've got it!"

"You got it, boy! Get that fish!" My father yelled back. I pulled harder and harder on the pole, and as I did my Uncle Tim realized that the boat rocked with each one of my pulls. My "big fish" turned out to be the boat. The fishing line had wandered underneath and made its way to the other side. My dream of catching the biggest fish of the day ended with laughter and humiliation. My father, however, enjoyed the event and would share it with everyone once we were home. This time, our fishing trip didn't create nearly the same excitement.

We went to Miami for New Year's Eve. During the day, we went to South Beach and watched my cousin and brother try to surf. The water must have been about fifty degrees, yet they were determined to give it a shot.

We had dinner at Hooters in Miami, and the scenery out of the windows was unbelievable. The women who were serving us in their skimpy orange and white outfits were alright, too. I didn't want to leave because of the beautiful Miami women serving me hot wings. Although having parents with you and trying to pick up women isn't the best combination.

After we ate, we went down to the Orange Bowl parade, because the college football national championship was in Miami that year. We watched the floats for a few minutes until we went to see my cousin's girlfriend, who was singing in a bar. She was only sixteen, but her father knew the bar manager, and she was singing for the New Year's Eve show.

The evening ultimately ended without anything eventful happening, and I had spent another New Year's Eve without a girl at my side. This was the first New Year's Eve that I had spent with my family since I left home after high school. The year before, when I was in Pensacola, I had stayed in Florida because I didn't have enough time off to go home at Christmas. Now, despite all the people who were around me, I felt lonelier than I had in a long time. I shook off the feeling and turned my thoughts back to my dreams of attending the Academy. This helped my mind to refocus on what was more important in my life.

My thoughts led me back to the Prep School and the challenges that were ahead of me. It sometimes felt like I was alone while I suffered at the Prep School, but all along, much like during New Year's Eve, I really had family there to support me whenever I needed it.

seven

•SHOW ME YOUR FRIENDS AND
I'LL SHOW YOU YOUR FUTURE•

. . .

"Friendship is born at the moment when one person says to another: 'What! You too? I thought I was the only one.'"

- C.S. LEWIS

Although I continued to study over Christmas break, I was unable to figure out a single trigonometry problem on my own. Back at school, the third quarter was beginning, and I was ready to take on a new role in my academics. Despite my fears, within the first week of math class I was getting the hang of trig. I even began helping one of my friends in the class. Mrs. Porcelli was our instructor. She was in charge of teaching the "special" students in the third quarter of the Prep School.

All of Mrs. Porcelli's students started the quarter feeling as if we didn't have a chance of going to West Point. But after the first class, her style of teaching renewed our faith in the instructor system. She made everything easy, and I began to work ahead of the lessons. She was supportive and very kind to the students—she was also a civilian. Perhaps that had something to do with it, but that kind of support was something that was unfamiliar territory for me. I really didn't have any stupid questions for her. She answered anything I asked, and usually with a smile on her face. A trusted advisor with a positive approach? It wasn't until years later that I learned that people learn in several different ways—through fear or through positivity. I learned quite a bit from the fear of my first two instructors, but my learning was elevated by Mrs. Porcelli and it was all through her positive approach. Think about that the next time you are teaching something—a teenager how to drive, a subordinate an Excel function, or even coaching in Little League. Positivity enhances performance.

In two weeks, I had already completed all of the homework assignments for the quarter. I was used to working hard—to really struggling through each problem and sometimes spending hours on my homework. However, with every trig problem it became more natural for me to figure it out quickly and come up with the right answer.

I had to finish these problem sets early because I had started tutoring other students in my company. I focused on Randy Simon and Ryan Murphy, and they worked every problem under my supervision. During my first semester, I had not really made a lot of friends. In fact, in the second quarter I was the company first sergeant and had to enforce rules on my peers. It was quite a daunting task since I just wanted to fit in. This was a similar position to what I had faced in Florida, and I had come quite a long way since that time, but this time I didn't attempt some speech in front of the large group. I focused on providing leadership through my own actions.

Through my tutoring, I worked my way into a group of friends that Randy had been hanging out with all year. I had been so focused on schoolwork and basketball that, until now, my social life had taken a back seat.

I was still working at least six hours a day between classes on my own and also tutoring Randy and Ryan. Both of them were at critical points in their academic careers at the Prep School. Neither of them had passed either of their finals in the first semester; if either failed another, they would be kicked out of the school. They were actually doing worse than I was, and that was no small accomplishment.

I had worked so hard and so quickly that in four months I had completely caught up with four years of high school math. I was on my way to learning a full year's worth of trigonometry in four weeks. All the hours of sacrifice were paying off, and people were actually relying on me to help them with their homework. I was honored that people trusted me with their math problems.

Basketball had taught me something that will stick with me for the rest of my life. You put the hours in and you get results. It was a simple math equation that even I could understand at this point. With those results came confidence, the kind of confidence that you need to teach others and help people. It was when I became a tutor to others that I felt I was becoming a dot on the right—something I couldn't even have considered six months previously. Helping others is also another secret to this life that leaves us fulfilled. I originally did it to fit the cooperate-and-graduate theme that USMAPS has, but as I did more tutoring, I really loved helping other people. To this day, if I can help someone else achieve their dreams and turn them into realities, I'll do it in a second. That all started with tutoring at the Prep School.

Although I was still in the "special" class, I had shown much more promise that quarter than anyone had anticipated, including myself. I was still haunted by my first day of classes in both quarters, and that was propelling me to fulfill my dream of attending West Point. I was pulled aside by Mrs. Porcelli halfway through the third quarter. She let me know that she had signed off on my application to the Academy.

I was ecstatic with the news. Then she told me that, taking into account extra credit work, my grade stood at 101 percent. At that point, I had perfect scores on all the tests. I was accomplishing my dream with each day that passed, yet I still had my newfound friends to help, and I didn't want to let them down. I began a new regimented system of tutoring, a minimum of three hours per night, in order to get Randy and Ryan ready for the finals that quarter. Although this took away from my own studies, if I could master the material enough to teach others, that was greater than studying on my own.

We also had the SAT that quarter and had to prepare for that as well. I had worked through the SAT prep book five times and felt confident that I was going to do much better. The test took place on a Saturday, and I was ready to surprise the world with my score. Unfortunately, it was a surprise but not in the best way.

I had scored a 750 on my first SAT and knew I would improve. I had no choice. More than 90 percent of the people accepted to the Academy scored higher than 1200 on their SATs. Those who don't are generally athletes. I later found out that some people got above a 1500 on the test; some even scored a perfect 800 on the math portion. That amazed me, and I knew I would never perform so well. Even so, I paid twenty-five dollars just to hear my score early.

At a pay phone in the academic building, I nervously dialed the number to get my score. I hung the phone up and picked it back up again at least five times without completing the call, unsure if I actually wanted to know the results. My acceptance to the Academy hinged on this test. The importance of my score was excruciating. The instructors had drilled into our heads that we should be preparing for it all year long, and I had been. I probably studied that book more than anyone. I knew that I was as prepared as I could be, yet this test doesn't measure how hard someone works. It measures potential and current abilities.

I picked up the phone for the final time and listened to the automated voice tell me that I had scored a 1030 on the test. I was so disappointed that I found it difficult to motivate myself for anything else the rest of the day. I was sure that with that low of a score I wasn't going to be accepted. Then I ran into another student who told me he scored lower than that, and he was excited about it.

I asked how he could be so happy with such a low score and found out that regardless of our test scores, as long as we passed each quarter at the Prep School and got the necessary math and English teacher recommendations, we were going to the Academy. I was relieved, and my mood soared when it became known throughout the school that I was the student whose SAT scores had improved more than anyone else's.

It wasn't too hard to improve that much, especially when I started with the lowest scores in the history of the Prep School. After my first SAT, I had people ask me if I had taken the test drunk, or if I just didn't want to take it, and I always responded with the truth. I honestly didn't know how to do any problems on the test. It wouldn't have even mattered if I had brought a calculator; I didn't even know how to use one.

Amazed with what I now saw as a great score on this SAT, I went back to my regular studies and focused on my newfound loves of tutoring and hanging out with my new friends. We had also developed a new study method for each night before each test. It didn't consist of problems or any other usual study material. It was spiritual. All of us had seen the movie *Glory* more than once. As in the movie, the five of us learned to take our problems to God.

After we completed our studies the night before a test, it was out of our hands and into those of God. Just like in the movie, we started a low hum that began with, "Oh my Lord, Lord, Lord." The clapping of hands on beat with everyone else's would get us going. Each one of us took our turn in our prayer to God. Mine would always be: "Dear Lord, I go into battle tomorrow with a mechanical pencil in one hand and the HP 48 (our calculator) in the other. I want to thank you Lord, and let you know that if tomorrow is our great getting up morning and we should fail, I want you to let our families know that we went down standing up. That we looked our problems right in the eye and let them know we weren't scared. Thank you, Lord. Thank you."

"Oh my Lord, Lord, Lord," would begin again, and the next person would take his turn. When we each had had our turn, silence would fall over the room, and each one of us would look the others in the eye with a nod of approval and leave the room to get some sleep before the next day's test. We did this ritual with every math exam, and even before the first test of the third quarter. It was powerful. It represented everything about the Prep School that I love to this day. We were having fun, motivating each other to be the best we could, and bringing the spiritual side to it. I loved every moment of that singing ritual when we were doing it.

Randy and Ryan went into that first test, completed the problems, and turned their tests in with a confidence they had never felt before. They came back and told me they were positive this was going to be the first test they had passed all year. Sure enough, Randy scored a 90 percent, and Ryan scored an 80 percent.

We celebrated that weekend by going to the Officers' Club on post. It was the morning of St. Patrick's Day, 1998, and we found out that the majority of the people who went for the brunch celebration at the club were more than seventy years old. Regardless, my friends Randy, Ryan, Eddie, Paul, Terry, and I were determined to have fun with the people there. We had brunch, and a few of the guys had some Bloody Marys after the previous night's usual outings. We were a rough bunch, but the older ladies were enjoying the music, and we thought it would be nice to ask them to dance. They accepted. It wasn't music made for dancing fast, but Celtic music and stuff by Frank Sinatra. (I guess most of the people there were Irish or Italian.) We had champagne and talked with the veterans, who spoke of their lives in the military and how rewarding the experience had been.

We spent several hours with them, and some of them told stories about World War II. Another guy told us of the Korean War and what it meant to him. Regardless of which war they had been in, there was one underlying fact that they spoke of most frequently: the bond they formed with each other. My friends and I couldn't yet relate so far as the bond of war was concerned, but we had been through our own war with academics, and we had come out on top. We looked at each other and knew that we would all be friends for life.

We finished that day at the Officers' Club with a newfound love for our profession-to-be. We were excited at the idea that someday we might be leaders in combat, much like the older gentleman we had met that day.

One man spoke of a specific battle in Bastogne, when he was with the 101st Airborne Division. He said that his unit was surrounded by the Germans, yet none of the soldiers around him gave up. They motivated each other with thoughts of seeing loved ones again and the promise that, when they got back to the United States, they would all get together someday and tell stories about what they had been through.

I looked at him, wondering if I would face something as dramatic as he did, though Prep School definitely was proving difficult in its own way so far. I was lucky making the friends I had made, because we formed something more than a bond. We had become a family, one that provided the support we were all looking for. We had become brothers, and, although not through combat, we shared a time when we had been at our lowest. We were there for each other, just as if we were birth brothers.

eight

·BROTHERLY SUPPORRT·

. . .

"Sometimes being a brother is even better than being a superhero."

- MARC BROWN

My brother, Brian, had supported me my entire life without my even knowing it. I am sure this is the way he wanted it.

Brian is a year older than I am, and when we were younger, he always seemed to be a hundred pounds heavier and a foot taller. When we were growing up, my father and mother fostered a rivalry between us in every sport and in every competition. I believe that they did this to create closeness between us, and, over time, it did. We are closer today than we ever have been, and it all started with the sports rivalry. Sports were the easiest thing to get us riled up about, but my father would even create push-up competitions between us, with money going to the winner. The push-up contest called for fifty push-ups in sixty seconds. I was the first one to do fifty—managing that total in thirty-seven seconds. I pocketed fifty bucks.

It didn't help that my entire family has a competitive nature that would drive away most outsiders. My parents created an environment that constantly drove me to be better in all facets of life. My father always told me that if I did it right the first time, I wouldn't have to do it again. Brian, for his part, seemed intent on making me into either a better basketball player or a legitimate crybaby. Either way, he would beat me into submission on a daily basis in our one-on-one basketball games.

Then there was football. My brother and I would spend hours practicing with my father, who played quarterback while we ran pass patterns. During baseball season, we had backyard home-run derbies. With his height and weight advantage, Brian won every time. We even joined a bowling league when I was in fifth grade and competed for the best bowler in the league trophy. I still taunt him with that.

When we were in high school, the competition between us never ended. Brian lettered in three varsity sports as a freshman, and my jealousy reached its peak. I knew that by making the varsity teams, he would become a popular guy. That bothered me even more. I was not popular and was at an age when that was important. As a freshman, my brother was reaping the benefits of popularity from his athletic prowess. I was just trying to grow to be five feet six.

In eighth grade, I began my journey to become the greatest basketball player in the world, and my brother was there every step of the way, trying to defeat my dream.

As I sat on the freshman basketball team, Brian laughed at my inability to play the only sport in which I participated. He knew that humility would force me to try harder. Our sibling rivalry increased with every year, and my skills never seemed to keep pace with his. We earned the same grades, so I couldn't even beat him in academics. My sister, the genius in my family, was almost a straight-A student, thus increasing the difficulty of beating anyone in my family at anything.

Being driven comes from somewhere in your life. For me, it was my siblings. My sister was incredibly smart and beautiful, and my brother was an amazing athlete. I was a scrawny kid who hadn't found his way yet. In my head, I like to believe I was the ugly duckling turned into a beautiful swan, but in reality I just kept going until things were done. I was resilient, I had grit, I had no clue how hard things were going to be for me—these are all things that can't truly be measured by a test and that was my specialty.

When I was a junior in high school, and Brian was a senior, we were both increasingly popular. My newfound ability to play basketball and my brother's steady wrestling skills (he made it to state championships twice) earned us a story in the county paper with the headline "Brothers Lead the Way." My mother was excited, and she bragged to the family about how her babies were interesting enough for a full sports story. She actually ended up being quoted in the article more than we did. Although the article was about my brother and me, everyone loves being in the paper. My brother and I didn't care that she got in on the act. We were both excited, about the article coming out, and our anticipation of the issue grew until the day we got the paper at the local store.

I opened the paper and laughed so hard that I couldn't bear to show my brother. I had to put it down and gather myself so he wouldn't beat me senseless. The paper had run a picture of me that took up more than half of the front of the sports page (I decided at this point that I was the better-looking brother, so I deserved it). On the next page, they showed a picture of Brian at a wrestling match he didn't even wrestle in. It was only two inches big, a tenth the size of the picture they used of me. I couldn't help but laugh at my brother. The article had equal portions about both of us, but if anyone knows anything about news articles, it's all about the pictures.

It was about this time that Brian and I decided to go outside and play basketball one-on-one to settle this thing once and for all.

I was a starter on the basketball team by this time and was third in the city in scoring. Brian really didn't have a chance of beating me. However, the rim in our backyard was only a little more than nine feet high, and he thought he could just power me in and score at will. For the first time in our one-on-one history, I took a commanding lead from the beginning. We always played to ten points. It was nine to one and I had the ball. I gave Brian a fake to the left and cut back right without hesitation. My brother fell to the ground as I dribbled by him and dunked the ball with both hands. I hung onto the rim as I stared him down.

"That's for all the times you beat me!" I shouted. I felt a sense of satisfaction and pride so overwhelming that I could hardly keep it to myself. I let out a scream of joy, and my brother left the court without looking back. I was proud of myself because I knew all of my hard work was paying off, yet I didn't want the competition with Brian to ever end. He single-handedly pushed me harder than any other person in my life, and he didn't even know it.

Brian graduated high school and continued to live at home while I finished out my senior year. He was a great athlete in high school, but his grades held him back from getting any worthwhile scholarships. He decided to wait until after my basketball season to give wrestling a try at Ohio State. He became discouraged with both school and wrestling, however, and quit after one semester.

When he was still living at home, he attended all of my games. He was secretly my biggest supporter. He wouldn't yell when I scored or when I hit a three-pointer to win the game. Maybe I was wrong. Maybe he knew he was my inspiration and drove me to play better.

At a game against Bethel High School, a conference rival that my parents had attended, I scored twenty-seven points and led our team to victory. Brian and his friends were leaving the gym when he heard five guys making fun of me. He turned around and confronted the lead guy.

"What the fuck did you guys say about Swanson?"

"Fuck that guy," the first one replied. "He's a piece of shit."

Without a second thought, my brother picked the guy up by his throat and threw him more than ten feet. He landed in a pile of trash.

"Anyone else think Swanson's a piece of shit?"

The remaining boys scurried away, leaving their friend knocked out in the trash pile. My brother's friends laughed at the poor kid. He had messed with the wrong guy.

Brian never told me the story, but all his friends approached me the next day and retold the story with jealousy, saying that they wished they had someone care that much about them. I knew my brother had always cared about me, but we had always been so different in personalities. For the first time, I felt that we were going to support each other instead of cutting each other down. It was then I knew Brian and I could count on each other for anything.

After high school graduation, I continued down my path to the Army, while Brian still struggled with what he wanted to do in life. He moved to Cincinnati, and I went to Fort Jackson for basic training, then down to Pensacola for my AIT. While I was in Pensacola, Brian and I talked to each other over the phone, but we never had a lot of time for each other. He still supported me and surprised me by saying he was proud of me. After all the years of secret support, his words meant everything to me.

After AIT ended, Brian lived at home in Nashville, Tennessee, with my parents, who had moved there at that point. That's where Brian was when he learned I had been accepted to the Prep School. He said he was happy for me, but I could tell that he was also a bit jealous. It reminded me of the newspaper spread, the one in which I received a majority of the attention. I didn't want the tension between us to escalate, especially since he was the person who motivated me to work so hard. Brian didn't look at it that way, and before I left for Fort Sam Houston in Texas, he barely acknowledged me. When I was home on leave, we didn't go out like we had before, and this bothered me. I thought we were past the teenage jealousy years, but as I found out, sometimes that phase never passes.

I stayed in Texas for a few months, and Brian and I rarely talked.

I missed him, yet I didn't want to be the one to give in to this petty game between us. I went to the Prep School without knowing what my brother was doing and how he had been. I had so many things on my mind that I didn't have the time to worry about anyone else except myself.

Brian and I started talking again after I had been at the Prep School for several months. We started to laugh and joke again, and things were becoming normal. We spoke a lot about the upcoming Christmas break and our road trip to Florida to visit our relatives. I also told him about starting on the basketball team, and he said he wished he could see me play. I told him the Army-Navy basketball game was the biggest game of the year and invited him to come. The game was in February, so that gave him over four months to plan a trip to New Jersey. To my surprise, he agreed and said that whatever it took for him to make it to Fort Monmouth, he was going to do it.

I asked my parents if they wanted to attend the game since Brian said he was coming, but due to their work schedules, they weren't going to be able to come. My sister declined as well. Brian was the only one to see me play that season, and he came for what turned out to be one of the most exciting basketball games in the history of the Prep School.

When we started the game, I noticed that Brian wasn't in the stands. I was upset that he had told me he was going to make it to the game and then didn't show up. Then, halfway through the first quarter, Brian and his two friends walked through the door. I was energized by his presence and began hustling more than in any other game the entire season. Brian was finally going to get to see me play at the Prep School. Despite all the effort, things didn't pan out. I played horribly. I played a majority of the game, but didn't do anything for the team. I missed several shots and turned the ball over a few times. All I really wanted was to make my brother proud of me. I accepted my poor play, and as we went into overtime, I found myself sitting on the bench for the remainder of the game.

The game itself had been exciting, but as a player if I did poorly, I found it difficult to pay attention to the rest of the court. I was selfish in that manner, but I disappointed myself more than usual because my brother had driven more than ten hours to watch me play.

We all get caught up in our own actions sometimes. Even as part of a team, we start glaring at our own weaknesses, and it is selfish to do that. I rarely have that mindset today, but I did while I was at the Prep School because I didn't want to be singled out as the reason why we lost games. No one wants to be the scapegoat for anything—in games, in business, in life. The only way to not be that person is to properly train, study, and work prior to the event. That's it. Prepare and prepare some more to ensure there is no question of your work ethic when it comes to the event. This is not being selfish. This is being the ultimate team player.

We won in triple overtime, and our tiny Prep School crowd went wild. When our coach released us, I went to talk to Brian and his friends. They told me I did great. It was a nice gesture from them. I knew I had played badly.

We were going out that night before they headed back to Cincinnati. Brian kept any bad comments to himself and said he was happy for having gotten the chance to see me play basketball again.

I didn't go out too much, but I wanted to take Brian somewhere decent. We went to the neighboring town of Red Bank and had dinner at a local diner. After that, I remembered that we had a group of comedians coming to the Prep School. I thought this would be a good show for Brian and his friends. My brother understood that back then I didn't drink or go out partying. We had a good time at the show, and when it was over, Brian and I spent time just talking and enjoying each other's companionship.

I had seen him at Christmas, but our time apart seemed like years. I learned at the Prep School that time away from family is extended. The weeks are like months, the months are like years, and the years are like decades. We talked about our past and shared funny high school stories. We discussed all the issues that were going on with the family. Everything seemed to be working out for the both of us, and we were genuinely happy for each other.

This was the first time in our lives that we didn't fight about anything, and our support for each other grew with every passing day. Since Brian had agreed to come to this game, I thought I would invite him to my graduation. He reluctantly agreed to come. He wasn't sure if he wanted to make a trip like that one again, but if it meant that much to me, he would.

His decision to show up for my graduation meant the world to me, and he also agreed that he would prolong his visit so that he could spend graduation weekend with me at our cousin Tracey's house in Long Island.

A brothers' bond is weird to say the least. It changes over time, for better or for worse, but it changes. I no longer look at us and think about competition. I look at us and think, *How can I be his biggest cheerleader in life?* When you are young, you say things and do things that are horrible toward each other because you are around each other *all the time*. When you get older and live away from one other, like we have, you don't have time to fight. You just want to have a good time and celebrate life's victories.

nine
·SPRING BREAK·

. . .

"Spring is nature's way of saying, 'Let's party!'"

- ROBIN WILLIAMS

At the Prep School, we had two breaks during the second semester. One was an official spring break, and one was a four-day weekend. After the basketball season ended, all I had to worry about was graduating from school and not doing anything that could get me kicked out. The four-day weekend was coming up at the end of March and I wasn't sure where to go until my mother suggested that I go to Long Island to see Tracey and her husband, Jay.

It took my old roommate, Rob Stoffel, and me several hours on trains to get to Traccy and Jay's place in Setauket. Every quarter, you switch roommates at the Prep School—at least I did—and it gives you perspective on how to adjust to different people. Luckily, there is a train station called Little Silver just outside the Fort Monmouth gate. It took us into Penn Station in New York City. From there, we took the Ronkonkoma line out to Setauket. Rob and I were eager to make a good weekend of it. Until now, I had never drunk any alcoholic beverages. That, however, was about to change.

Tracey had grown up about forty-five minutes from my family. Our extended family, including Tracey, her brother Phil, and a collection of cousins, used to get together on the weekends to play football. My mother is Tracey's godmother, and so we always had a special bond with her. She married Jay when she was twenty and moved out of Ohio as quickly as she could. She settled in Long Island. I was thankful for that because, throughout my time at school, I went there to spend time with her and Jay. The most recent time prior to spring break was my Thanksgiving vacation when I helped Jay put Christmas decorations up and bottle homemade beer. I don't even put Christmas decorations up at my own house today, and I have never brewed a batch of my own beer either. Needless to say, new experiences are always good for anyone.

Tracey picked us up on a Thursday night, and before we made it to her house, she asked what Rob wanted to drink. He started drinking in the backseat before we even got home. As soon as we dropped off our bags, Jay was ready to go out, so we didn't eat dinner. I had consciously made the decision that I was old enough to start drinking and that I would be responsible about it.

We arrived at a bar named Tara's during happy hour and were buying drinks for ten and twenty cents. Tracey bought my first drink, a Captain Morgan and Coke. She asked how it tasted. I thought it was pretty good, and next thing I knew I had drained the glass like it was a regular soda. Tracey asked why I had drunk it so fast. I didn't understand what she meant until I turned my head toward Rob. My vision blurred, and I felt my whole body tingling with heat. My first "buzz" had begun. I liked it. A lot.

I started throwing down the Captain and Cokes until Tracey had to stop me. I didn't get ridiculously drunk, and we ate at Tara's so my buzz went away. We went to several bars after that, and I became a test dummy for all the drinks that Tracey, Rob, and Jay liked the best. I had problems with the taste of beer, so I stayed away from that—it would take years to acquire a taste for it. When we went home, Rob finished off his case of beer.

I woke up the next morning—I guess it was actually around three in the afternoon—and, still in my pajamas, I began drinking again. That night we went to another country bar, where a friend of Tracey's was singing. Before I knew it, I became good friends with the White Russian.

I noticed that the female lead singer of the band was attractive and, though only on my second night of drinking, liquid courage dictated my behavior. In addition, several older women had grown quite fond of me. I was doing a country line dance with them while the song "New York, New York" reverberated from the jukebox.

I learned that night how to act like a complete jackass in front of an audience. Regardless of how annoying I had become or how petulant I acted, I still made an attempt at the lead singer, who obviously had seen me making a fool of myself.

I had confided to Rob that I was going to make my move after she finished her last set. He agreed that I should say something. It was clear even in my drunken state that she wanted to talk to me. I was concocting the perfect line to use on her. When the time came, however, I wasn't all that eloquent.

"If it wasn't for you," I slurred, "I would have left this country bar a long time ago."

She laughed, either at my line or at my drunken stupor. She kept talking to me, and I was apparently putting on all the right moves. She gave me a ride to the next bar where I would meet up with Jay, Tracey, and Rob. She gave me her number and told me to call her the next time I came to town (I tried calling it the next time I visited Long Island, and it was the wrong number). I was so excited that I could meet a girl while I was drinking. Now, I was starting to figure out why just about everyone drank. Liquid courage was the best friend of unconfident men all across the world, and I was now another satisfied customer of alcohol.

Rob and I spent the rest of the weekend eating well and drinking like there was no tomorrow. Tracey still loves to tell the story of how she was the first one to get me drunk, and I am happy that she was the one to be there.

Jay and Tracey were perfect hosts throughout the whole weekend. There were drinks, women, and music at all the bars where we went. I only hoped that my spring break in a few weeks would go as well. I was going with Ryan to Houston, Texas, where we would spend the weekend with his family, and I wasn't sure how things were going to turn out.

Weeks later, when we arrived at Houston Hobby airport, the Murphys were overwhelmed with joy to see Ryan and me. At the airport, I ran into a girl I knew from AIT in Pensacola. I said hello to her, but didn't get to visit with her long because Ryan's parents were waiting on me and I felt Ryan's impatient stare.

We hopped in their Ford Expedition. As the Murphys asked me questions, Ryan nudged me and told me that I had to call his parents "sir" and "ma'am." I thought he was joking, but we were in Texas, so I wasn't going to question how his parents raised him.

I later learned that this is proper protocol for everyone's parents I would meet throughout the West Point process. Even after adults tell you to call them by their first names, a cadet or cadet candidate must always refer to his seniors as "sir" and "ma'am." Over the years this became second nature for me. I still use that etiquette with any friend's parents I don't know.

We arrived late on Thursday night, and in the morning the Murphys took us out for lunch. They paid for everything. It was Easter weekend in April, and we only had a few days before we had to go back to the Prep School. We drove around Houston, and Ryan took me to meet an ex-girlfriend. I soon learned that he always seemed to have a girl for himself, but not for anyone else. In this situation, however, this girl introduced me to a friend of hers, and we hung out for the majority of the weekend. On Friday night, Ryan's parents took us to a Garth Brooks concert, where we sat in the seventh row. We were so close that when Garth was singing, we waved to him as he pointed back at us.

The weekend was turning out to be one of the best of the year, because the Murphys supported us and were genuinely happy that we were there as part of their lives. The next morning, Mrs. Murphy scheduled a manicure appointment for us (I know, manicures for men). She had already paid for the appointment, and at fifty dollars for each of us, we reluctantly went along with his brother, Joe. The three of us had our manicures. I honestly felt that I could never be more spoiled than I had been in the past two days.

As we left the nail shop, I looked at Ryan's fingers. Somehow, Joe and I made it out of there without any problems. Ryan, however, had a shiny coat of clear nail polish on his fingers. We made fun of him for a long time afterward, and Ryan found himself still scratching that coat of polish off months later.

We had a quiet dinner Saturday night and went to church the next morning to celebrate Easter. Mr. and Mrs. Murphy even put together a basket for me. They filled it with an inspirational leadership book, candy, and five plastic eggs, each containing a twenty-dollar bill. They gave me a hundred dollars, and they had only known me for a few days. I couldn't believe their generosity in everything they did for me that weekend. They had become my surrogate parents. After that weekend, I began to call them on a weekly basis. They told me they were going to be at graduation to support Ryan and me. It was the first time in my life that someone else's parents cared as much about me as Ryan's did. I didn't want to let them down.

As a parent now, I realize that the Murphys didn't have to treat me so well. As my children get older, the Murphys set an example for me that I would like to follow when it comes to my children's friends. Be kind. Be giving. Be like another parent. They will always remember that kindness.

The Murphys were forever grateful to me for tutoring Ryan in math class. I had enjoyed the whole process of tutoring him and Randy because, if I could teach someone else how to do something, it meant I had mastered the material. Thanks to my own quest for self-preservation, I not only learned the material but also gained confidence in my ability to teach others.

After that weekend, Ryan and I grew closer and began to trust each other with everything. As the weekend ended, my thoughts turned back to the Prep School. I thought of our Commandant, and his recognition of my struggle throughout the year.

The Commandant stated in one of our earlier assemblies, "Look around you. About half of you won't be here for the graduation this year. That's based on previous classes' records."

The Commandant had spoken a lot of truths throughout the year, and he was one of the basketball team's biggest fans. I couldn't wait for my chance to get to talk to him one on one.

ten

•FOURTH QUARTER•

. . .

"We can't have full knowledge all at once. We must start by believing; then afterwards we may be led on to master the evidence for ourselves."

- THOMAS AQUINAS

By the fourth quarter of Prep School, I had established myself in the battalion as a hard worker and someone to be emulated. Although other people found this obvious, I could only see that I still had plenty of room for improvement and was a long way from my goal of graduating from West Point. I felt that I still had something to prove.

I have always loved the movie *Rudy*, and my favorite line comes when the janitor and Rudy are overlooking the football field near the end of the movie. Rudy wants to quit before the last practice of the season. The janitor, however, tells him, "You're five foot nuthin', a hundred and nuthin', and you ain't got an ounce of athleticism in you. You hung in with the toughest football team in the country for two years, and if you haven't proven anything to yourself yet, you ain't ever gonna do it."

I probably had a better shot at reaching my goal than Rudy did, but I identified with him every time I watched the movie. I know the heartache of chasing a dream. Just getting into the Prep School had been a dream to me, and finishing it was beyond my wildest dreams.

I had had one key supporter since day one: the Commandant himself. I had already reached the Commandant's List, which meant that I had a B or higher in English and Math. Making the list had become a dream of mine soon after I arrived.

As part of a fourth quarter assignment, we were to interview anyone we chose and explain their stand on the topic of our choice. That assignment was the least of my concerns.

On an early April morning, I walked over to the big man's office. I had only been there twice, and both times were for negative counseling with Maj. Kirby, who was in charge of the Department of Military Instruction. However, this morning there was more substantial work to do than getting yelled at about punishment tours. I was the battalion "XO"—the executive officer—which meant that I was in charge of punishment for the cadet candidates. This time, I was here to talk to the highest officer in our battalion, and the best part about it was that he had always been kind to me because of his big support of the basketball team. It also helped that his son was on the team. I knew he would be friendly and the interview would go well.

The Commandant greeted me as I entered his office. Every colonel's office has pictures and memorabilia of previous units in which they have served. The Commandant's office was no different.

My eyes scoured each individual picture. I was taken aback by his twenty-seven years of service and all of his accomplishments. I secretly wanted to make the rank of colonel one day, but at this point I was barely managing the rank of cadet candidate.

The Commandant had the manner of someone who had been interviewed many times before. I could picture in my mind all the other cadet candidates who had come before me and gawked at all the awards and encased colors from units all over the world. After I complimented the Commandant on his decorations, he was ready to begin the interview.

I asked several questions about Bosnia. The Commandant gave

me the politically correct answers, knowing that regardless of what he said, I would write a flattering piece about him. I wasn't bold enough to write a paper about our commandant that was in any way critical when I hadn't even made it out of the Prep School yet (I would save disobeying an officer's orders for the Academy).

We finished the interview and continued talking about the Prep School and how proud he was of our class. He told me that he was following our class to the Academy, where he would become a math professor. I was overly happy at the thought of having a familiar face at the Academy and, maybe even more importantly, a solid supporter who could help me through hard times there.

As all this sank in, he said, "Dave, I want to show you something." He grabbed a thick folder devoid of any markings and handed it to me.

"Open it up, and tell me what you see."

I slowly opened the folder and thumbed through page by page. Looking at the names on the sheets before me, it wasn't hard to figure out that it was the roster of our class at the Prep School. Some names were highlighted. I kept flipping through until I reached my name.

It was highlighted. I looked at the Commandant. He could probably read the worry on my face.

"Do you know why your name is highlighted?"

I looked away from him with shame. "Sir, I'm not really sure why I was one of the selected few." I didn't know, of course, what I had been selected for, but I feared it wasn't good.

The Commandant paused a minute and then spoke. "You're highlighted as one of the fifteen people who would never make it through the Prep School, one of the people the admissions department didn't want to give a chance." He told me to look back through the list and see if I had noticed anything.

I slowly went through the list. My hands trembled. I was afraid he was about to tell me that my dream was over. I was afraid he had the power to say I would never make it at the Academy, and that I didn't even deserve the chance to go. I put my index finger by each highlighted name and looked back at the Commandant for confirmation. Once I got back to my name, he nodded.

"You are the only one on that list who is still here at the Prep School."

A shiver went up my spine, and I realized that, based on the Prep School's attrition rate, I had defied the odds and was still standing. The Commandant added, "And you're the only one on that list who will make it through the Academy. I believe in you."

Those four words have followed me throughout life. When someone is positive to you and states their belief in you, be around that person as much as you can. Positive thinking will last for years, while negative thinking lasts for just a few minutes.

I wanted to thank him for his support throughout the year. I was excited that I was not only proving myself to my academic instructors and the basketball coach, but also to the admissions department at the Academy. I wanted to shout with joy, but the Commandant continued with his speech.

"Dave, you have been a joy to watch this year. I talked with your instructors, and they told me that you put forth more effort than any other student in their classes. They all wish they could teach more students like you, who are eager to learn and willing to help anyone. The Academy needs people like you, people who aren't naturally strong in academics, but who have sheer will and enthusiasm. You will succeed at West Point, and, without a doubt, you will succeed in life."

The Commandant dismissed me from his office, and I thanked him for his kind words of encouragement. He said I should never thank him; he should be thanking me for being the ideal student and a model for others.

I walked out of the Commandant's office with my head higher. I was prouder of my achievements then than at any other time in my life, including when I was playing basketball. I knew Prep School had challenged me in every facet of life, and I had persevered. I hadn't run back into the house at the first sight of adversity. I stood my ground and faced all the goats that came my way. I couldn't wait to let my family know that my acceptance to West Point was pretty much secured.

Until the end of the year, every cadet candidate still awaits an appointment from the Academy's admissions department. I was not able to get a recommendation from my senators or my congressman, but Prep School students don't need one. Completing the Prep School with good recommendations from the instructors is enough to get any Prepster into the Academy. I had never been happier.

I was on my way back to my room after my visit with the Commandant when Maj. Kirby stopped me. In addition to being in charge of military instruction, the Major also volunteered with the basketball team, so I had grown to know him pretty well throughout the school year. We had developed a special, but positive (in my mind), relationship because he was our home basketball game announcer, and when I finally started in the games, he would officially announce me as "Old Man Swanson." I was a little older than the other students there, but the main reason for the nickname was my balding hair style. I had been going bald since I was seventeen and had grown used to the idea of being bald for the rest of my life.

Maj. Kirby was one of those officers who liked to pick on his favorite cadet candidates. Since he was a major, no one said much back. I learned early in my military career that speaking up was a good thing when done with tact. I allowed Maj. Kirby to take his cheap shots at me, however, without much retaliation.

It's difficult to explain this sort of relationship, especially when you're the subordinate. In the Army, these relationships exist all the time. Some leaders are motivators, others are yellers, and some even tease their subordinates. I learned to live with Maj. Kirby's comments.

When I was returning from the Commandant's office, Maj. Kirby pulled me aside. Before I knew it, I was in his office. Maj. Kirby started the conversation by telling me to shut the door and take a seat. In all my time on the battalion staff, he had never asked me to shut the door and sit down. I expected that this was going to be an elevated teasing and that I would leave with my head down. Our conversation, however, failed to meet my negative expectations. And it also let me see Maj. Kirby in a new light.

"Well," he said, "I just came back from a recruiting trip at some posts."

Intrigued, I asked, "What posts did you go to?"

"The posts are irrelevant," he said. "I wanted to tell you what I told them about the Prep School."

I remained silent and let him finish, because this was the first time he hadn't called me "Old Man" and actually looked like he wanted to mentor me.

"I told all the young soldiers out there about your story. I told them your academic scores before you came here, and I told them that you were the most successful turnaround story this Prep School has ever seen. I found myself talking to all of these specialists and below and realized that with your hard work and determination, anything is possible in life. You have displayed that more than any other Prep School student that has even been through here."

He shifted in his seat a bit, then stood up and gazed out his window and said, "I just wanted to say thank you for your efforts."

He dismissed me. I left his office unable to believe what I had heard. First, we actually had engaged in a conversation without him offering any ridiculing comments. That amazed me. Second, although I agreed that I had worked hard all year, I knew that each year there were people just like me—people who gave all their effort. I wasn't anything special. I couldn't have been any better than any previous students. I was only an average student in my own eyes.

It was at that moment that I changed my feelings about Major Kirby. He had recognized my efforts. I didn't receive an award for it. He just said thank you, and that was more than enough for me.

Recognizing someone for their hard work is something we don't always do in life and in business. A simple "thank you" can mean more than any printed-out certificate of achievement. If you have the ability to tell someone thank you for your efforts on a daily basis, then do so. It doesn't have to be just at work either. It could be your spouse, your children, your colleagues. They all appreciate hearing a thank you from you.

I wanted to think about my conversations with the Commandant and Maj. Kirby. I felt the need to contemplate what they had said to me, but above all, I was excited to know that I was already accepted to the Academy.

eleven
•COMMUNICATION•

. . .

"I speak to everyone in the same way, whether he is the garbage man or the president of the university."

- ALBERT EINSTEIN

I hurried to the battalion dayroom, anxious to call home and tell my parents I had been accepted to West Point. The dayroom had a phone center, a television, and a ping pong table. With such little entertainment, I became pretty good at ping pong. I'm no Forrest Gump, but I am decent. I never had time for television, and I made phone calls only when necessary.

Over the course of the year, the phone card companies made so much money at the expense of Prepsters that my parents got an 800 phone number so I could call without it costing me anything. This was before the cell phone rage of calling after seven p.m., so I did my usual weekly calls after church on Sunday.

Midway through the year, however, I began to notice that one phone always had a line of at least five or six people. Around the holidays, the line was even longer. There was a little secret about the phone that had not been released to everyone. It was always the same people waiting in line, and during the middle of the second quarter, I finally asked one of the guys in line why they always waited for that phone.

I had been studying so much that my common sense wasn't the sharpest it had ever been. One cadet candidate told me that the phone was a "free phone." I mentioned earlier about "free" things in the

Army and that they are never as they appear. The first time I waited in line, I dialed directly to my parent's house without a phone card or an operator. I was amazed, and so was the rest of the battalion.

The free phone became the hit of the Prep School, and soon, everyone was using it. It was so great that there were even officers and enlisted cooks who were using it to call loved ones all over the world.

I recall several people calling their boyfriends or girlfriends in Germany, Japan, and England. These were the international callers. As long as the dialer had an international code, they could call anyone in the world.

I didn't know that the phone wasn't meant to be free. I somehow thought that the phone was an MWR (Morale, Welfare, and Recreation) phone meant for long-distance calling. By the end of the year, everyone—and I mean everyone—in the school had used the phone at some point. Little did we all know that our graduation hinged on our use of that phone.

It was this phone I used to call my mother and let her know that I was definitely accepted to the Academy. She congratulated me and reminded me of the conversations we used to have when I was younger.

Ever since I could remember, my mother had always been supportive and told me that any dream I had was possible, and that she and my father would be there for me whatever the case may be. After my first operation to place tubes in my ears, the doctor told me I wasn't allowed to go outside because it could damage my hearing. I was worried that I wasn't going to be able to play sports again, and, as always, my mother was there to comfort me. She let me know that I would be able to do whatever I wanted when the time came.

By the time I was ten years old, I had glasses and braces, and I had undergone ten operations in the ears and throat region. After all that, I asked my mother, "Why does God hate me so much?"

My mother was astonished. "David," she told me, "God doesn't hate you. He's just making you special for the rest of the world to notice."

I liked that answer a great deal. My mother always had a way with words, an ability to smooth over any situation that wasn't pleasant with euphemisms. I wondered how she was going to describe the difficulties of the Academy so that I would enjoy them.

Soon, the Commandant called a class meeting in the auditorium. When we arrived, he was holding an invoice and wore the angriest face I had ever seen on a usually kind man. He began the meeting with several options, such as not letting the class graduate or making everyone in the class pay his portion of the phone bill.

As he prepared to tell us how much the phone bill was, a cloud of shame settled over the crowd. The student body became more silent than I had heard it all year, just as the Commandant yelled, "$52,416! $52,416 is the bill that YOU guys ran up over the course of the year, on the MCI phone in the battalion dayroom."

The Commandant shook with anger. More than anything, he said he was upset that no one had reported the free phone to him earlier than a few weeks before graduation. We all stared at him and wondered, would you really give up a free phone in our position? We all confirmed by nods and looks that he couldn't fail an entire class because of a phone bill, so logically, what would happen was that the tactical officers would take the names of those in battalion and report them up the chain of command.

As the tactical officers called students into their offices, they realized that everyone had used the free phone at some point. Even some of the officers had to report their own names up to the Commandant.

Over the next week a dismal funk fell over the battalion because of the free phone incident. Everywhere, small groups formed to whisper about the phone. English instructors made it the subject of essays in

order to incorporate one of West Point's most important values—
honor—into our minds. The honor code at the Academy stated that
a cadet would never lie, cheat, steal, or tolerate anyone who had done
any of those things. The weight of the world, it seemed, lay upon the
Commandant. The outcome lay solely in his hands.

I began to worry that all of my hard work throughout the year—
all of my studying for class, and all my struggles on the basketball
court—in the end would count for nothing. I felt discouraged that,
despite all my efforts, I still might not go to the Academy. A year
earlier, West Point was beyond my wildest dreams. Now those dreams
were within reach—or had been before the phone became an
obstacle. I couldn't believe that something as trivial as a free phone
controlled so many destinies.

Our concerns increased the week before graduation. Everyone
seemed to believe that, if we didn't bring it up, maybe nothing would
happen. The Commandant was asked daily by various students
about our immediate futures. We wanted to know as soon as possible,
but the Commandant ignored our concerns and wouldn't address
the issue. Finally, I learned why he wouldn't say anything.

The Commandant had worked out a deal with MCI, the phone
company, to drop the charges. He had always regarded our class
as the advanced guard for West Point's bicentennial class of 2002,
the one that would graduate two centuries after Thomas Jefferson
established the Academy. He couldn't let anything happen to us.
He reminded MCI that none of this would have happened if
its phone hadn't been defective. I will always feel a little guilty,
however, because I know that the Commandant recognized the fact
that we should have known better. In hindsight, maybe we were a
little defective, too.

As a leader, doing the right thing when no one is looking is called
personal courage, in the Army and elsewhere. Having the personal
courage to not make those phone calls is what we all should have done,

without question. However, as you gain more experience and you lead more people, you realize personal courage is something that is admired by everyone. Doing the right thing, all the time, without question is absolutely difficult to do, but at the end of the day, you live with your own conscience and that is what is going to allow you to sleep at night—or that is what is going to keep you up, staring at the ceiling.

Finally, the Commandant called another assembly. We all had the same thought: if we didn't pay the bill and graduate, we would ultimately go down as a legendary class. There were classes before us that had famous or infamous incidents that made them legendary. If our class pulled this off, we would become part of the tradition of the Prep School screw-ups. This might someday seem funny to others, but to us it was deadly serious. It was our future.

"I decided that this class has learned its lesson with the free phone incident," the Commandant told us. "You all understand that honor should never be questioned, and integrity is a man's character." Without another word, he turned and left the room.

As the doors closed, smiles lit up the room. We hugged each other and slapped our fellow cadet candidates on the back. Some cadet candidates even high-fived each other. These must have been the ones who had made the international calls.

The Commandant looked out for us, the way a leader takes the hits, so his subordinates don't have to. It was a subtle moment of leadership that I didn't quite understand at the moment, but as I spent time in combat, that became my philosophy. I would do whatever it would take to keep my soldiers from getting harmed if that was possible. Mission first: people always.

I jumped up and went to make a call from one of the regular phone booths. I decided to let my parents know that everything was still going well, and the free phone incident was finally over. The next thing we had to worry about was graduation. It was coming up fast.

twelve
·GRADUATION AND BEYOND·

. . .

"We don't stop going to school when we graduate."

- CAROL BURNETT

I had finally made it. I had survived the Prep School, and I
could hardly contain my joy.

In our final week before graduation, everyone focused on
summer break and not on West Point. We talked about where we
were going and what we were going to do. Ryan and his father
had invited our small group of friends to their ranch house on
the Guadalupe River in Hunt, Texas. We were excited and had
plans to do nothing but sit near the river and drink with our
closest friends. The trip was only going to last four days, but the
anticipation of it had carried us forward for months. The phone
incident was now a thing of the past, and the only thing we had to
do was to entertain family until graduation was over.

The night before graduation, we had the traditional formal
dinner. Everyone was dressed in Class A uniforms with bowties.
The officers wore their dress blues. The dinner was a gala held at
the Fort Monmouth Officers' Club. The social hour went well. The
prime rib dinner was perfect, and because graduation was the next
day, no one was going to get too inebriated. The dinner ended.
As battalion XO, it was my job to give the awards to the officers
leaving the Prep School.

Maj. Kirby was first on the list for the awards, and I decided it
was time to pay him back a little for the taunting that many of us

had received throughout the year.

I began by telling the crowd that everyone at the Prep School loved Maj. Kirby. This was a lie, but it sounded good to all the parents who were at the event. "One day, on the way to basketball practice," I told them, "I saw Maj. Kirby running in his physical training uniform. At first, I had to check again because I didn't really think he was that big, but it sure enough was him."

I heard all the cadet candidates let out a quiet "OOOOOOOO." The class knew I was about to lay it all on the line. We had all had enough of his torture, and someone needed to make fun of him.

"I watched Maj. Kirby for five minutes," I continued. "He had made it about 200 meters, and I was going to ask him if he needed any help getting home. Instead, I watched him suffer through the running. I sat back and enjoyed the pain that he endured with each step. The award we got him was a plaque, but I think we should have gotten him a pair of running shoes, because the ones he owns won't allow him to run fast enough to pass the PT test!"

The crowd erupted with laughter, and I felt pretty good about getting back at Maj. Kirby. He came up to get the plaque, but refused to say anything to the student body. My words apparently bothered him, and I later learned that, as I told the story, he turned red in the face and balled up his fists. Everyone at his table laughed along with the story. Everyone that is, except him. He probably wanted to kill me for what I said. Everyone came to me after the speech and thanked me for what I had said about him. I was getting comments like, "It's about time," for the rest of the evening, but I made sure to avoid Maj. Kirby. He continued to glare at me from a distance. It was uncomfortable, but I had finished the Prep School, and had just gone through one of the toughest years of my life. That was his satisfaction. For many years, I basked in this moment. Today, I recognize that I shouldn't have done that. I respected him. Hell, I even liked him and he liked me, too. I guess all of his comments and teasing had finally led to that moment.

At graduation, I met everyone else's parents. Togo West, the Secretary of Defense, was our guest speaker. I don't remember anything he said. The ceremony was held outside of the post's auditorium. We were all in our Class A uniforms, and it was again hot enough outside to melt the shoe polish off our leather shoes—a fitting reminder of our first day when we'd arrived to a scorching heat. The bleachers where we sat were white and blinded everyone in the crowd. This deterred any parent from trying to get a close picture of his son or daughter during the ceremony.

No one from my family could attend the graduation, and I started to realize that accomplishing dreams didn't mean much unless there was someone there to share them with you. Both of my parents were working and were not able to attend, so I spent my time with Ryan and his family, who had opened their home to me earlier in the year. They welcomed me in, since Ryan had told them about my tutoring him throughout the second semester.

This was a great time in my life. I had passed my classes, started on the basketball team, saved more than $10,000, and made lifetime friends. I was proud of myself, regardless of who was there for me. As the graduation ceremony ended, the year's events replayed through my mind. I remembered back to the beginning, when the entire class was laughing at me. I felt an indescribable sense of pride known only to others who have sacrificed as much as I had that year.

My brother had showed up earlier in the year to see the Army-Navy basketball game and had agreed to meet me at graduation and drive with me to Jay's and Tracey's in Long Island. Unfortunately, Brian didn't show up until three in the morning following graduation. By this time, I was already ranting and raving about my family's lack of support.

I got a ride with another kid from school, and he took me to Long Island. As soon as I arrived, I began drinking with my cousins. I had wine, beer, shots, and mixed drinks. The pain I was feeling wouldn't last long, especially with my cousin Phil there. I celebrated my graduation all afternoon. By the time we went out at eight p.m., I was already beyond intoxicated. That, however, didn't stop Phil from buying me fourteen shots at the bar.

After the fourteen shots we left the bar. Later, I would learn that I was grabbing girls' butts on the dance floor. It wasn't exactly the choir boy image that I had portrayed throughout the school year. On the way out to the car, I started a fight with a guy who was twice my size. I had the liquid courage, of course, or at least I did until Tracey dragged me away. We arrived back at the house, the safest place for me to be. Only then did my brother finally arrive.

I hugged Brian forever, and his girlfriend realized that it wasn't going to be a good night for me. I don't remember what I said, but I ended up in the backyard with Brian. I couldn't fight the tears when he asked me what was wrong. I started with everything about the Prep School and the sacrifices I made that no one, not even he, knew about. When I told him that my friends had become closer to me than my family, he grew angry. I told him I wasn't talking about him. I began furiously, loudly, talking about my parents. That eventually led to the neighbors yelling at me to shut up. Tracey had to drag me back inside before they called the cops.

I don't really remember what was said. It was evident that I was so upset about my parents' not attending that I had drunk myself into oblivion. I was disappointed that they weren't there to share that moment with me. I really felt that my year at Prep School had been a great achievement. Perhaps I hadn't adequately shared the amount of enthusiasm I felt when I told them about the graduation.

As Brian and Tracey dragged me back into the house, Brian held on and let me know that everything was going to be alright. He told me that everything was going to work out between the two of us and between me and our parents. He had always protected me from everything, and that night wasn't any different.

I woke up on the couch the next morning with the biggest headache of my life. It was eleven in the morning, and I wasn't sure what had actually happened the night before. All I knew was that I had to find some sunglasses and a hat for Tracey's outdoor party that was happening in a few hours. Brian chose to forget everything I had said the night before, and we have never brought it up. The rest of the weekend found me alcohol-free and yearning to go home and relax in Nashville for a few days before I went on my trip to Texas.

After those days in Nashville, Eddie and Ryan met Randy and me at the airport, and we flew together to San Antonio. Ryan borrowed his father's Ford Expedition and, during his week off, had joined Hunt's Volunteer Fire Department. I am not sure what he and his friend actually did for the fire department, but they both received a blue light that would allow them to hurry to a fire without the police stopping them. It was a sound idea in theory, but with four twenty-year-olds in a car, every event seemed like an "emergency."

On the way to the ranch house from the San Antonio airport, we pulled over several "speedsters," and Ryan, the newly appointed Texas Ranger, let them off with a stern warning and then we continued on our way down the road. After we did this trick several times without any problems, we lost interest. We realized that we would have more fun in those four days than in the rest of the five weeks of break combined.

We arrived at the ranch house in Hunt and started drinking as soon as we had the chance. We were going to meet Ryan's grandparents the next day, because they lived in the nearby town of Kerrville. Partying was still our priority for the evening.

Nonny and Papa (pronounced Pah-Pah) arrived in the afternoon after we had spent the better part of the morning drinking by the river. Ryan's dad, Bill Murphy, showed up and grilled steaks for us. Everything was right in the world. We had just sacrificed a year at the Prep School, and now we were getting treated right. Papa knew that I had tutored Ryan at school, and he pulled me aside and told me all his World War II stories. He let me know that he was once General MacArthur's driver. He was extremely proud to have served his country. Ryan never actually told me that he was related to Audie Murphy, the most decorated soldier in the history of the Army. However, his grandfather's story about being General MacArthur's driver led me to believe that there was a connection.

Papa's talk of duty, his pride in America—all of it inspired me and reminded me I couldn't fail out of the Academy. I was somehow able to survive the Prep School, but the plebe year at West Point promised to redefine sacrifice, and I could only hope I was up to the challenge. In a few weeks, however, I wasn't going to have a chance for such self-reflection.

By the time we finished our dinner, several local girls Ryan knew had shown up at the house. The local girls washed the dishes quickly so we could go back down to the river and drink some more. While we were all heading down to the Guadalupe, we decided we needed more to drink. Ryan and I went to the liquor store and picked up some bottles of vodka and orange juice. As soon as we got back to the river, we poured out half of the orange juice, replaced it with vodka, and mixed it up. All five of the guys from Prep School promised to stay there until it was finished. Only then could we go to the local bar.

It was then and there that we all made a pact: in four years, as graduates of the United States Military Academy, we would all meet here again. When we did, we would do this same exact thing with our class rings shining in the setting Texas sun. This thought inspired all of us to get back to the Prep School. From there, we would go straight to West Point and wait for our new hell to begin. We had never been more ready.

thirteen
•HELL'S BEGINNINGS•

. . .

"I hated every minute of training, but I said, 'Don't quit. Suffer now and live the rest of your life as a champion.'"

- MUHAMMAD ALI

We all arrived back at the Prep School two days before R-Day, or "Reception Day," as it was called in the letters West Point sent to our parents. With all our gear still in our bags, we prepared ourselves for Cadet Basic Training, better known as "Beast Barracks."

We had a barbecue in the quad at the Prep School the day we got back, and it was great to see everyone again after the summer break. The evening was filled with laughter as everyone exchanged stories of what we did on our five weeks off.

As the night wore on, talk turned toward Beast and how all of us were going to get split up. All of my friends would be spread throughout the Corps of Cadets, and I wasn't sure how often I would get to see them.

In my year at the Prep School, I had met many people that would affect me for the rest of my life. Some had pushed me positively and negatively, but all contributed to my life. They helped me prepare for West Point's different challenges I was about to embark upon.

Except for the random outburst of laughter from a cadet who either didn't care or didn't want to think about the pain we were about to endure for the next six weeks, the bus was silent on the way to West Point. I kept to myself, thought about the next few days, and what I had just been through.

The friends I had made at the Prep School helped me keep my motivation at times when I thought I could no longer push myself. Randy and Paul continued to be my friends from the first moment we met in Cadet Candidate Orientation. We had lived close to each other throughout the majority of the year, and we would spend our weekends together if we had the chance. I started to realize that our chances of living near each other were quickly coming to an end.

It was an exhilarating, yet frightening, experience without having all the support I was used to at Prep School. However, the comfort of having Rob go to West Point made the transition easier. He was a solid friend who had been with me since the beginning of the most difficult year of my life.

My basketball teammates, Joe Peppers and Charles Woodruff, gave me inspiration to be ready for the basketball season when it came around. Charles had become my workout partner at the end of the year for basketball when he didn't assist me with homework anymore.

I continued to go to Sunday choir with Josie through the entire year. We became great friends and continued to support each other in academics. She became a person to depend on for support if needed.

All of my friends' and family's support pushed me through the best and worst of times. As we arrived at West Point, I didn't focus on what I had accomplished individually, but rather the term "cooperate and graduate" that Sgt. First Class Sutton had introduced to me earlier in the year at the room inspection. I determined that if I was going to make it through Prep School with this philosophy, I needed to apply it as soon as we all stepped off the buses at the Academy.

It was the day before R-Day, and the 110 graduates of the Prep

School took a couple of buses to West Point to get situated before the other new cadets began to arrive.

At the Academy that night, we stayed in empty cadet rooms, and no one bothered us, but it was difficult getting to sleep that night. My anticipation of getting Beast Barracks over with plagued my thoughts.

I knew what was about to take place, and I couldn't do anything about it. I had to think about each painful moment as it happened. I couldn't predict anything except my next formation. I laid in my bed staring at the ceiling until we had to get up at four.

Then it began. We had morning formation, ate breakfast, and walked to the football stadium with the rest of our classmates.

Once again, we remained quiet as we grabbed seats at the stadium. I sat next to a friend of mine, Shaun Marzett, who had been a manager on the USMAPS basketball team. We watched in silence as a cadet made her way to the front of the area and began her speech, which was tailored to the new arrivals rather than the Prepsters. She mentioned issues with our parents and what we were about to go through. She was trying hard to remember the lines she had memorized the night before, and before I knew it, she said, "You now have ninety seconds to say goodbye to your parents."

All the Prepsters looked at each other and started laughing. We didn't have our parents there, nor did we need time to say goodbye. Shaun and I hugged each other and pretended to cry as if we were leaving each other for good.

This was our first day at West Point, and we Prepsters were already making a name for ourselves by making fun of the brigade adjutant. She felt stupid about what she had just said to us, but quickly realized that she was the upperclassman and had control of all of us.

"Move your asses," she said.

We looked at each other and questioned her authority. Did she know what we had just gone through for a year? Did she have any clue how close we all were to each other?

Apparently, the other upperclassmen didn't care what we had recently faced and overcome. Their smirks hinted that our recent victories were only a warm-up, and that hell's beginnings were headed our way.

•LIFE LESSONS
CHEAT SHEET•

50 Tips to Finding Your Path

**CONSIDER THESE QUESTIONS AND TOPICS WHEN WORKING
TOWARD YOUR BIG GOALS.**

IDENTIFY THE INFLUENCE THAT GAVE YOU THIS DREAM
Was it in your formative years?
Recall the specific event.
How did it make you feel?
Who encouraged it?
Who told you no? (If they didn't, you would be doing it now!)
How did you get off the path?
Which behavior did you consistently choose to get there?
What did you learn from the wrong path?
What were your emotions and reflections on that wrong path?
What was the moment that told you it was wrong?

IDENTIFY YOUR WHY
Be clear about why you are doing this.
Your Why is what people will buy.
Your Why will wake you up and drive you.
Your Why has to be constantly reminding you.
Your Why needs to add value.
Your Why needs to be genuine.
Your Why needs to recall your best emotions.
Your Why is about others.
Your Why determines your true value.

MAKE THE DECISION

Decide. Right. Now. Then don't look back.

Deciding is based on not good but great information.

Deciding is well thought out.

Deciding is not determined by external events.

Deciding is reconfirmed with your Why in mind.

Decisions are clean.

Decisions cannot be fickle.

Decisions require confidence.

Decision is made. Time to go all in.

IDENTIFY YOUR HOW

Plan it out.

You're in an apprenticeship, regardless of age.

Look at others' plans.

Timing is instrumental.

Thorough analysis is required.

Don't allow paralysis analysis to be confused with progress.

Get resources aligned with your plan.

Help on figuring this out is okay.

Starting from scratch should be your last resort.

Find similar people on the path

Coaches and mentors can save you years.

HAVE MANY QUESTIONS

Get the answers you are seeking, don't settle.

Genuine networking.

Honesty is best policy (tell them upfront: I want to do what you do).

Consider, how can you help them?

Be authentic in your expectations.

Let them help shape your plan.

Respect them from the get-go.

Have a book idea?

Contact us at:

info@mascotbooks.com | www.mascotbooks.com